HIGH OVER BOULDER

5th Edition

A HISTORICAL GUIDE TO ROCK CLIMBING NEAR BOULDER, COLORADO

By

PAT AMENT
and CLEVE McCARTY

Preserves the history,
gathers the best routes, easy or hard

David Breashears leading Rain, in Eldorado / photo by Pat Ament

Dedicated to the
the early climbers,
with all their integrity,
who ascended among these rocks
for the beauty,
joy, and friendship
they found as well as brought

Published by TWO LIGHTS

4990 Osage #D-12
Boulder, Colorado 80303
(phone: 303-494-4829)

ISBN 0-9648606-0-0

Cover photo: Colin Lantz on Your Mother, Eldorado

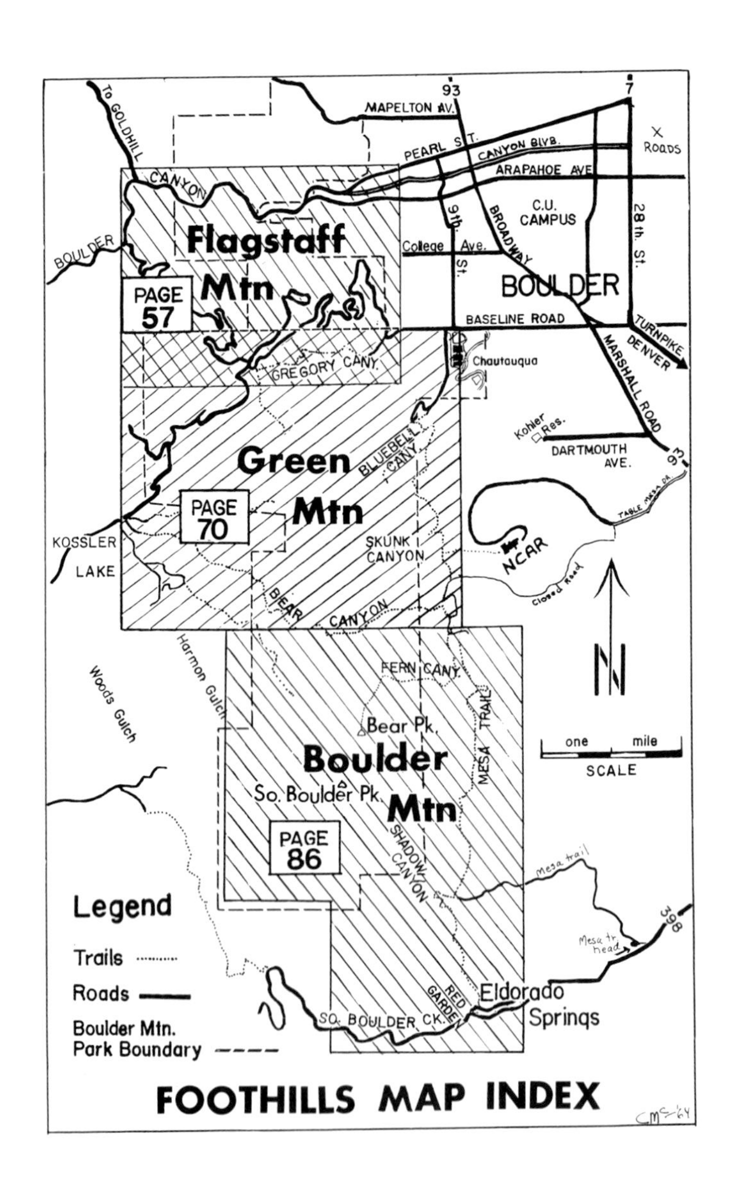

93
7
To GOLDHILL
MAPELTON AV.
PEARL ST.
CANYON BLVB.
X Roads
ARAPAHOE AVE
CANYON
C.U. CAMPUS
28 th. St.
9th. St.
BROADWAY
BOULDER
Flagstaff Mtn
College Ave.
BOULDER
PAGE 57
BASELINE ROAD
TURNPIKE
DENVER
Chautauqua
GREGORY CANY.
MARSHALL ROAD
Kohler Res.
DARTMOUTH AVE.
Green Mtn
BLUEBELL CANY.
93
PAGE 70
TABLE MESA DR.
KOSSLER LAKE
SKUNK CANYON
NCAR
Closed Road
BEAR
CANYON
Harmon Gulch
Woods Gulch
FERN CANY.
N
Bear Pk.
one mile
SCALE
MESA TRAIL
Boulder Mtn
So. Boulder Pk.
PAGE 86
SHADOW CANYON
Mesa trail
398
Mesa tr. head
Legend
Trails
Roads
Boulder Mtn. Park Boundary
RED GARDEN
Eldorado Springs
SO. BOULDER CK.
FOOTHILLS MAP INDEX
CMS '64

CONTENTS

HIGH OVER BOULDER -- 5TH EDITION

Introduction, by Pat Ament

It is not the purpose of this guide to catalogue every route that has been done. The routes spoken about in this book were the first of note in the area or, being of later and more recent times, are those that add to the history by some uniqueness, power, or essential personality. A few of the routes described are pivotal to an era, or to the current era. Some are the most difficult in the area, while many are included for the reason that they are favorites for their beauty -- in some cases simple or moderate yet having a quality that has been a fascination to generations.

The majority of routes in the Boulder area have at least some beautiful aspect. Choosing involves a responsibility, which I am willing to take based on the years of experience I have had with the rock formations near Boulder. Opinions differ, and certainly there are many worthwhile people and climbs not here mentioned. I have tried to avoid pointless, rinky-dink, or overly contrived routes, and routes that are dangerous. Of course any route can be dangerous if the climber is not the measure of it. The areas covered in this guide are Boulder Canyon, Flagstaff Mountain, Green Mountain, Skunk Canyon, Dinosaur Mountain, Fern Canyon, Bear Mountain, Eldorado Canyon, and the Mickey Mouse area (above Eldorado to the south). There are many good areas around Boulder to climb, but these hold the true history.

I am grateful to Bob Culp who read the opening historical "chronology" and offered suggestions. He and I perhaps are the only two who have stayed continually active in climbing from the late 1950's until the present. We thus have followed the history and know it. Roger Briggs, who has thrived as an active genius of rock climbing in the Boulder area for over three decades, offered ideas for this book. Christian Griffith and Bob Horan shared with me their thoughts and photos. I spoke with Colin Lantz, who told me about several of the new sport-routes. Jim Erickson reflected about his best climbs. It was a pleasure to speak with Dr. Harold Walton and listen to his accounts of the Maiden, Cussin' Crack, and Hornsby's Ledges. Tom Hornbein spoke with me, to my benefit, as did Mark Taggart who made me laugh as he remembered his first ascent of the Maiden. This book owes tribute to every individual who has, over the years, contributed information to the various editions of High

Over Boulder or who has, with stories, climbs, or photography added to the lore. I am especially appreciative of my eternal friend Tom Frost who enthusiastically supported this project and who has believed in me in all my efforts. My best friend, my wife Robin Ament, helped proof-read the history and offered suggestions.

As a boy, I was impressed with Cleve McCarty's ascent of the 53 fourteen thousand-foot peaks in Colorado in 53 days. When I decided on my own, while in ninth grade (about 1961), to write a rock climbing guide to Boulder, Cleve already had gathered information about the history of the trails and about rock climbing in the area. His research had started nine years before mine when he found himself at the end of his 120-foot ropes, hanging in space, on a 150-foot rappel. Creativity was needed, as well as a guide. Learning of my desires, he approached me and proposed we join forces. I loved reading Layton Kor's letters to me, with written accounts of climbs. "This is a pritty route," Layton wrote.... Cleve and I climbed the Bulge, in Eldorado, and Cleve stopped on a foothold now and then to speak into a microphone connected to a tape-recorder he carried in his pack... When the 1st edition was near completion, Cleve joined the Air Force and went to Germany! For me to contain my youthful exuberance and wait those years for him to return was a test. He sent an occasional sketch he found time to do. Five editions of High Over Boulder have helped us stay in contact through the years, as did our mutual friendship with the late Baker Armstrong bring us together on occasion. When I realized a desire to attempt this latest (and probably last) approach to High Over Boulder, Cleve -- in a psychic way -- had begun thinking a few of my thoughts.

As has been the goal of this book, we wish to write about the spirit and beauty of climbing and the history as much as tell about routes. We hope to create a book that can be read for enjoyment as easily as it serves to lead one up the best climbs. The research in the various editions of High Over Boulder has provided the bulk material for several other guides. Cleve and I have never been selfish in letting that be so and have seen those successes as a positive by-product of our efforts. In some cases, our errors were corrected. Guides are a process almost like folklore and evolve for the better with input from readers. It amazes me how much climbing has been done in this area and by so many. I look with respect at the accomplishments of every generation and in this edition have tried to be less judgmental as to philosophies that differ from my own. Individuals are reflected in what they create, and I am aided in my awareness of those achievements by writing about them. It has been a blessing for me to live close to the Boulder mountain terrain for so many years and to have the association I have enjoyed with climbers. The beauty, history, and people, even the clever names of routes, continue to bear, for me, a mystery and happiness that I never have felt so fully elsewhere. Because I grew up among these rocks, they are symbols of youth's freedom and remain for me an evidence of times that have been the best life offers.

First ascent of Sidereal, Skunk Canyon / photo by Dan Hare

ONE HUNDRED YEARS OF SUN AND ASCENT (AND OCCASIONAL RAIN)

A History of Rock Climbing Near Boulder -- By Pat Ament

So beautiful, and having a sentient strength, the natural environment west of and above Boulder, Colorado, inspired the early residents of the area to protect it. By virtue of wisdom and vision, much of the terrain immediate to the area was purchased and preserved as a "Boulder Mountain Park." This began in the 1890's when Boulder acquired Flagstaff Mountain. City attorney Charles N. Cambel drafted an Act Of Congress and presented it to Boulder's congressman. The land was granted to Boulder to be kept as a mountain park which might be rendered accessible by construction of roads and shelter but otherwise left in a natural state. Then Green Mountain and a portion of Bear Peak were acquired at $1.25 per acre. Several hundred more acres were purchased in such a way. Many years after, in the mid-later 1970's, Eldorado Springs was purchased as a state park.

Except for the possibility of Ute or Arapaho Indian ascents of the flatirons, the history of rock climbing around Boulder began in about 1898 with the Colorado Chautauqua Climber's Club. The name of the group was at some point changed to the Rocky Mountain Climber's Club, incorporating in about 1910 under the state law of Colorado. Activities included a few short hikes and steak-fries, and individuals of note included Eben G. Fine, Dr. Hungerford, and Mary Sabin. One of the organizers of Denver's Colorado Mountain Club, Sabin got her start with the Chautauqua Climber's Club. The first recorded ascent of the Third Flatiron, likely via the east face, was made in 1906 by Earl and Floyd Millard. A figure of Boulder climbing history, Ernest "Pa" Greenman, a surveyor who would become known for his trail building, care of forests, and his "101 ascents" of the Third Flatiron, joined the Rocky Mountain Climber's Club in 1914. Interviewed by Cleve McCarty, Greenman described the early 1900's: "People would come out from the east coast and the prairie states, and the first thing they wanted to do was to climb a high mountain. Those old, fat schoolmarms followed the schedule (the graduated program), and by the end of the year they were ready for Longs Peak."

Swede Rudolph Johnson, in a 1923 *Trail And Timberline* (a small journal published by the Colorado Mountain Club), wrote, "In climbing either flatiron (the First or Third) with a party, I have always used a rope, and it has been a life saver several times, but the first man up or the last man down gets no advantage of the rope. As to footwear, I prefer wearing hob-nailed boots, but have found rubber soled shoes, or even stockinged feet to be satisfactory...." Ralph Squires, president of the Rocky Mountain Climber's Club in the early 1900's, notes that most climbers in those days scorned the use of a rope. Paul Blanchard sometimes climbed at night, with a flashlight in his mouth.

In 1925, Charles Morris, poet/philosopher from Chicago, along with an unknown friend, is said to have climbed Shirt Tail Peak -- high above Eldorado Canyon to the northwest. Morris reported that the ascent went "straight up the face" and that devices he called "pitons" were placed during the ascent. The name of the rock was derived when they posted a wooden stick at the top and tied a shirt to it. Baker Armstrong in 1927, at age 20, climbed the Third Flatiron with Ernest Greenman (who then was 48). They carried only a 30-foot length of window sash cord and went up the rock in eighteen minutes. In 1930, Baker climbed the Third at night, an event which made the newspaper. The ropes were manilla. Baker's shoes were Keds -- high-top, soft-rubber basketball shoes that stuck well to the rock. There were no pitons or hammers. Climbers moved with the rope between them, holding it with their hands for occasional belays, unanchored. Much climbing of an unprotected nature was done, for example by Ronald Ives in 1934 up the Dog's Head Cut-Off route on the upper backside of the Third Flatiron. Descriptions by Ives of his ascents in the *Trail and Timberline* documented virtually every hold and exertion required to gain that peculiar, steep passage.

Easy distance to excellent, solid sandstone or granite, and routes with an abundance of holds, made Boulder one of the best places to climb. Cracks and ledges, continually interesting angles and positions of rock, stimulated imagination. Pines, dynamic weather, clouds of a celestial pink at sunset, their orange and reds, air blowing, wildlife, hawks, eagles, falcons, pigeons, meadows beautiful with flowers... added to the exquisiteness of experience.

Eldorado proprietor Bill Fowler believed climbing took place in the late '40s or early '50s, including an attempt -- he was certain in the '40s -- of a spire south of Eldorado seen near the skyline two rocks north of Mickey Mouse. Rumor had it that this ascent used techniques such as "back against feet." It was not certain

Early climbers reach the summit of a rock near Boulder
(the second highest person is the boy Baker Armstrong)

whether the climbers succeeded. To quote Fowler, "I can remember back to the '40s when our patrons would go out in tennis shoes and get hung up on the cliffs. You'd get a hunk of lariat rope and go up around back and come down. The earliest fatality was about 1942 when a couple was climbing on that thin, thumb-like spire near Rincon. The boy fell."

An interesting climb took place on the North Face of the Maiden, a spectacular spire, on October 26, 1944, by Roy Peak and Mark Taggart. Mark had joined the Colorado University Hiking Club, and friends said, "There's an interesting rock over here. Let's go look at it." He saw the Maiden and wanted to climb it. A freshman at Colorado University, he teamed with Roy Peak who was a senior at South High School in Denver. They trusted their lives to pitons and carabiners Roy made in metal shop, they wore tennis shoes, and the ropes were manilla. Employing a "safety pendulum" to cross a short, sheer section. The rope ran through a high piton, but supported them only lightly. They maneuvered upward and downward, in traverses, across the steep, north wall of the Maiden and, reaching the east ridge, attained the top. Taggart recalls, "I was scared climbing up the side of that overhanging, jutting rock near the end of the North Face." They then reversed the climb, scrambling down the east ridge, getting back onto the north face, and traversing west to the safety pendulum where they had left one of their ropes. Asked why they descended via the ascent route, Taggart added, "We didn't know any better. The only method then for rappelling was a 'body rappel,' the rope running between the legs, up the chest, and over a shoulder. I wasn't scared coming down." Taggart later received a letter from Roy Holubar who climbed the Maiden and thought he was doing a first ascent but found a small stack of stones left on top by Peak and Taggart. The stones surprised Holubar "to no end." The spectacular free rappel off the west overhang of the spire was first done by Brad Vandiver in about 1948. Tom Hornbein, who climbed the rock with another companion, belayed Vandiver.

Pianist David Hornsby and university chemist Harold Walton in 1948 pioneered Hornsby's Ledges up the north overhang of the Second Flatiron, undoubtedly the most difficult free-climb in the area at the time. Mistakenly listed as an aid-climb in later guidebooks, and claimed as a free ascent at 5.8+ (possibly 5.9?) in 1973 by Jim Erickson, Walton remembers that the route originally went all free: "Dave was the prime mover and led it. This was hard work, muscling up on those overhangs. More than once, one or the other of us fell and swung out. We pounded a piton up in the corner there. Ultimately we made it free, without using the rope for support." Walton also at this time climbed a high variation of the north face traverse on the Maiden, a variation later named after him. He noted that the variation was in fact led by Stan Gebura, another chemist. Walton said wrly, "It was good to find that 'thank-god' hold out there. Stan led the pitch. I was along, I know that." The "normally soft-spoken" Walton led Cussin' Crack on Castle Rock where he uttered a few words that were the derivation of that route's name. According to Walton, "We probably didn't make the first ascent of Cussin' Crack. I remember finding a piton in there."

Living at Chautauqua, Walton heard that a freshman at the university by the name of Pankey died in a fall off the First Flatiron. Pankey and a companion had scrambled ropeless up the flatiron and both fell. The companion caught himself on a tree. Contemplating this tragedy, Walton and a few friends at the university thought to form an organization whereby some education might be given to aspiring climbers and rescue might be provided for anyone in need. These friends, and their chief motivator Charlie Hutchinson, at that time Dean of Engineering, gathered at Ketchum Building on campus to meet and discuss the possibilities. That evening in 1948, they formed the Rocky Mountain Rescue Group. Ev Long and others previously, in the early 1940's, had formed the Boulder Search and Rescue, but it did not cohere into a solid group.

Also in 1948, Tom Hornbein -- a geology student at the University of Colorado who was destined to participate in the first American ascent of Everest -- climbed the Willy B with Bill Braddock. This small, difficult pinnacle south of (above) the Third Flatiron was a prelude to a famous ascent a year later (in 1949) of Northwest Passage by Bob Riley, Dick Sherman, and Hornbein.

The Northwest Passage followed a formidable line upward left across the north face of the Third Flatiron, downward, left again, up again, always on vertical rock, and then out a large overhang, arriving at the notch -- a square-cut opening on the upper right side of the east face of the Third. Soft-steel pitons, wafers, and army angles afforded dubious or little security both on the climbing and at belay spots. A pendulum technique was used for the second men (Hornbein and Sherman) as they crossed a steep, red slab ("Skid Row") climbed by Riley. After they failed to drill a bolt in rotten sandstone, they lassoed a point of rock in a crack eight or ten feet above. Riley prusiked to a place under the final overhang. After experimenting with ways to ascend the overhang, Riley managed to get in a piton. He lowered himself out from this and got in another piton. He suspended the rope to this second piton by tying a foot-loop in the actual climbing rope. Applying his weight to the loop, stretch in the rope sent him sinking into space below the roof. He was pulled into the belay stance at which time the climbers had the idea of creating an independent foot-loop from a separate sling to attach directly to the piton. This was perhaps the first use of direct-aid technique in Colorado, aside from the pendulum on the Maiden.

The yellowish wall of Friday's Folly, an exquisitely vertical route on the west side of the Third Flatiron, was climbed in 1950 by Tom Hornbein and Harry Waldrop and represented a bold level of free-climbing for the time. Hornbein recalls, "I was leading, and I was frightened. There were several removable holds." He used army pitons he and friends obtained by simply visiting a canyon west of Colorado Springs where army climbers trained and hammered pitons in all along the base of certain rocks. "We brought a crowbar and removed the pitons. There were hundreds of them."

On the flatiron rocks between Boulder and Eldorado, ascents were made that were the beginnings of serious free-climbing. The North Face of the Matron, for example, done by Karl Gustafson and Skip Green in 1951, was confirmed years afterward to be 5.6. Dale Johnson, in his first days as a beginner, with equally trained companions, attempted the south face of the Maiden several times without ropes. In the early '50s, Cary Huston led his infamous Huston Crack on Cob Rock. This slippery, short problem was a bit of a masterpiece for its day.

Roy Holubar hired a Colorado blacksmith to manufacture steel pitons harder than European Simond pitons or army pitons, and the first aluminum carabiners were produced by Raffi Bedayn in California. Hemp and manilla were replaced by stronger nylon ropes. A standard length of 125 to 150 feet could be purchased for under twenty dollars. Holubar Mountaineering and Gerry Mountain Sports soon were to serve the equipment needs of area climbers.

The first ascent of Cozyhang, on the Dome in Boulder Canyon was made in 1953 by Mike O'Brien and Jim Crandle. This was no easy walk-up and involved creative free-climbing -- including a blind traverse around a corner under a roof.

An October day of '53, Dale Johnson gathered with Dave Robertson and Cary Huston to ascend the airy, spectacular Northwest Overhang of the Maiden spire south of Boulder. Dangling high up under the overhang, with only space and tree tops far below, Dale placed a piton halfway into a poor crack. The next crack was smaller and worse. He hammered in a piton here only by the tip (driven in a quarter of an inch). Placing his weight into his foot-loop (aid-sling), the piton pulled. Dale flew downward into frightening space, hanging clear of the rock, caught by the rope and half-driven piton.

The Third Flatiron, while challenging hundreds of graduating rock-schoolers, sometimes was the subject of burlesque-like ascents. Dale Johnson, for example, in the company of Phil Robertson, ascended the east face of the Third wearing roller skates. Ernest Greenman led a blind man to the top. Baker Armstrong "walked up" the east face of the Third without touching the rock with his hands.

Inevitably Eldorado Canyon was discovered as a place to climb. Two U.S. Army climbers managed an aid ascent of the Bastille Crack in 1954 or '55. Redgarden Wall, via Redguard Route, was pioneered by Dick Bird, Cary Huston, Dale Johnson, Chuck Merley, and Dallas Jackson. With six hundred feet of climbing and two pitches of 5.8, this was a notable free-climb for 1956. Stan Shepard and Allen Bergen in 1957 aided what is now known as the Northcutt Start to the Bastille and went up the remainder of the crack free. Allen went first up the 2nd and 3rd pitches, without protection, scaring Shepard half to death. Bergen pulled some loose blocks onto himself one pitch from the top, so they retreated.

Cleve McCarty traverses in mountain boots in the early days of Eldorado

In the mid-1950's, six-foot-five Layton Kor, along with friend Paul Johnson, acquired a hemp rope, a few army pitons, and

climbed the Third Flatiron. This was Layton's first real climb. He notes in his biography *Beyond The Vertical*, "I had read an article in a popular magazine about a mountain guide who was guiding a client who fell. The guide was holding the rope and did the only thing he could in the situation, which was to jump over the other side of the ridge and counteract the fall. So I was on the alert for ridges to jump off should Paul fall." Kor soon climbed the steep Friday's Folly route on the backside of the Third, going first on the rope and gaining confidence in his ability. Kor learned of Eldorado Canyon and soon, in 1957, pioneered The Bulge with Ben Chidlaw, a Boulder lawyer. This was a significant ascent, involving four pitches of crackless, near-vertical climbing. Usually Layton tied into the rope by using a single loop of the rope wrapped around his waist and secured by a bowline. He placed no bolts and led 150 feet without protection past the high-angle crux. When climbers later protested that the route was too risky, having such poor (virtually nonexistent) protection, Layton hiked to the top of the wall, rappelled down, and using a hand-held drill laboriously hammered out a tiny hole and placed a bolt in it under the crux move. The route remains one of the area's best.

In 1959, Kor pioneered the Northwest Corner of the Bastille (with Pete Lev), the West Buttress of the Bastille (with Carl Pfiffner), T-2 (with Gerry Roach), and the Yellow Spur (with Dave Dornan), all requiring a combination of free-climbing and direct-aid. The Yellow Spur became instantly famous for its exposure, a quality emphasized by exuberant Steve Komito who fell from the final headwall and, caught by the rope, gazed head first down four hundred vertical feet of rock. Many individuals, somewhat of a remarkable procession, graced the Boulder region at this time with their presence and creativity, including Prince Wilmon who made a famous, somewhat arrogant statement that "There is no time in Colorado where you have to use a down-jacket." Wilmon died in a snowstorm on Longs Peak.

Ray Northcutt, a strong climber able at this time (1959) to do one hundred pullups (without dropping off the bar), was erroneously (or mischievously) told that Kor had climbed a 70-foot direct start to the Bastille Crack. Northcutt attempted to repeat it and, succeeding, created one of the best, most difficult, short, free-pitches in Eldorado -- the Northcutt Start, then given no rating but by today's standard thought to be 5.10d if not 5.11a. This may have been the most difficult free lead in America at the time. Only later, in 1960, did 5.10 arrive in California, with the ascent of "Dave's Deviation" at Tahquitz Rock by Tom Frost and Joe Fitschen.

In 1960, Kor and George Hurley climbed Eldorado's Grand Giraffe -- at its crux an overhanging chimney. They stepped on a piton and pulled on another. Bob Culp and Hurley climbed the route soon after, without stepping or pulling on any pitons. In retrospect, Culp noted, "It probably was no harder to do it without those little aids." Boulder climbers began quite early to use California's 5th-class decimal system for grading climbs. Doubting their abilities, they often under-rated climbs. In fact, Kor and a few others were as capable as the Yosemite elite. It was not uncommon for a climb rated 5.8 in Eldorado in the early '60s to escalate in later years to 5.9 or 5.9+.

On Flagstaff Mountain in 1960, Kor met Bob Culp -- the best boulderer in the area. Several friends, including Culp, Dave Dornan, Pete Lev, Stan Shepard, Deane Moore, Charles Alexander, and Charles Roskosz, became a loosely-formed group they called The Marmots. Whether or not Kor knew he was a member of the group or not was uncertain. He was their leader, at least indirectly, by way of the stimulus he provided. In Culp's words, "We got together for beers a couple of times." Roskosz had patches made up with a marmot head. These were sewn to coat sleeves. Culp wore his patch proudly until "it finally fell off." Dave Dornan put together a small booklet, the first climbing guide to the area, under the guise of the Marmots. Kor, with his height and energy, climbed swiftly over the Eldorado walls, free or with aid -- whichever was quickest. Free-climbing was important only if it facilitated speed, since the climbs of Eldorado generally were in those days thought to be training for longer routes on Longs Peak, in the Black Canyon, or in Yosemite. Kor brought almost anyone along who was willing to belay and to hazard the adventure. Among these companions were several not only willing but also competent -- such as Bob Culp.

Briefly employed as a store clerk for Holubar, Culp bouldered Jackson's Pitch, an overhang on the north side of Cookie Jar Rock, in his suit clothes one afternoon after work -- as witnessed by his awe-inspired, young companion, Pat Ament. Before bouldering was taken seriously or was viewed as a legitimate art in its own right, individuals approached it nevertheless with determination. In the '50s and early '60s, Corwin Simmons, Bob Beatty, Ray Northcutt, and Dallas Jackson were among the names heard in conjunction with difficult bouldering on Flagstaff. Bob

Culp, the most prominent boulderer in the early 1960's, had height, leanness, strong fingers, and a graceful style. He bouldered in Kronhoeffers, the best shoe of the day. Northcutt created the difficult Northcutt's Roll on Cookie Jar Rock, at one point falling from the rock into the road. Kor bouldered well also but rarely.

In 1962, Kor and Culp made the first ascent of Eldorado's most striking line, the Naked Edge. It had been tried previously by Stan Shepard and Bob Boucher, as well as others. During this time, Dan Doody -- a sales rep for Chouinard -- appeared on the scene with a trunk full of the newest creation: "Bugaboo" pitons. These were bought up quickly by Kor, Ament, Dalke, Culp, and others who enjoyed them as one of the delights of their secret culture.

Californian Dave Rearick, who had pioneered the Longs Peak Diamond with Bob Kamps, moved to Boulder to teach math at the university and soon, in 1962, made the first free ascent of T-2 with Culp. This was felt, among the area's small guild of serious free-climbers, to be a kind of breakthrough and, in a sense, was the landmark beginning of the free-climbing era of Eldorado. Also in 1962, Layton Kor led Psycho, in Eldorado. There existed on this route the danger of a long fall over a roof into space from the bold, vertical, unprotected 2nd pitch. Layton lunged at one point for a finger ledge. The route aroused the imagination and dread of climbers.

Layton Kor, Ruper Traverse, Eldorado, 1962 / photo by Charles Roskosz

In autumn of 1963, always revealing his energy and talent, Kor (in the company of teenage Pat Ament -- who skipped school at Layton's request) did one of the area's boldest leads yet, Rogue's Arete. Other than a forty-foot leader fall when a small foothold broke, Kor (unharmed by the fall) climbed with remarkable skill up this vertical and, near the top, sheer north face of Overhang Rock in Bear Canyon.

The mid and later 1960's saw difficult free-climbs in Eldorado and Boulder Canyon, not the least of which was Dave Rearick's 1964 free lead of the 3rd pitch of Athlete's Feat -- one of the first, as well as most strenuous, 5.10 routes yet done anywhere. Rearick had gotten a small "bong-bong" piton in halfway up the overhanging crack. Liebacking daringly above it, over the top lip of the crack, his foot slipped on a few grains of sand on the wall. As

he plummeted head first toward the ledge, Ament pulled in rope and stopped the fall with Rearick's head an inch from the ledge. Rearick knew that if he did not go back up right away the thought of what had happened would psyche him out. He led up the crack immediately and succeeded.

Also in 1964, Royal Robbins visited Boulder and free-climbed Eldorado's Yellow Spur with Ament. The two also pioneered the complete free ascent of Athlete's Feat in Boulder Canyon. The initial mantel-bulge of Athlete's Feat, rated 5.10 then and now 5.11a, was perhaps the most difficult free pitch in America at the time (aside from John Gill's short climbs and bouldering in the Tetons and in the Needles of South Dakota). Soon after Royal's show on the first pitch of Athlete's Feat, Ament -- still in high school -- repeated the climb, leading all the pitches.

Perhaps to answer these free ascents of T-2 and Athlete's Feat, Layton in 1964 free-climbed the West Buttress of the Bastille (5.9+) with Larry Dalke -- a previous first ascent of Layton's where he had used a few points of aid. Dalke, not only a good climber, was an excellent boulderer who performed as well in soft-soled Hush Puppies as in climbing shoes. Larry traversed and scaled the Boulder High School walls in his street shoes. On Flagstaff in the mid-'60s, he soloed the high boulder route Northcutt's Roll wearing Hushpuppies.

On a frigid, winter day in early 1965, wearing ear muffs and several layers of sweaters, teenage Ament (belayed by Dalke) led the second ascent of the scary Psycho pitch above the roof. On Kor's insistence, Ament placed a bolt a short distance left of the belay. This was to protect the belayer mostly, since the leader still had to make a long runout and risked a serious fall below the roof.

Ament on the 2nd pitch of Psycho, 1965 --
photo by Larry Dalke

After a few light-hearted attempts to top-rope a small, overhanging, quartzite crack in the west end of Eldorado, Ament in 1965 succeeded. The route had been discovered by Rearick and named Supremacy Crack by others who determined that it would be the most difficult pitch yet to be accomplished in Colorado. A year later, Royal Robbins visited Eldorado and climbed Ruper with Ament and Britain's Don Whillans. This day, Robbins introduced the use of climbing "nuts" to the area. The devices already had been in use in England for some time. In the hot afternoon following their ascent of Ruper, the three ambled over to Supremacy Crack. Belayed by Robbins and Whillans, Ament led the crack free. This was much more difficult than to top-rope, since protection had to be placed while hanging from one arm on the strenuous, overhanging hand-crack. Ament shunned the newfangled nuts and hammered in three pitons -- one every 10 or so feet. The lead was only slightly tainted by a few moments' rest on the third piton.

The first routes of a 5.11 grade, including Vertigo and Northwest Corner of the Bastille were done by Ament in 1966. The Vertigo and Northwest Corner ascents were questioned, in terms of style. Ament led the hardest moves of Vertigo free, without chalk and wearing heavy mountain boots, hammering in pitons that now protect the route. But he casually rested on a piton on much easier rock above... as though reverting back to Kor's mentality for speed or thinking that the free-climbing problem had been solved and nothing after that mattered. On the Northwest Corner, he began with aid up the crux headwall of the 2nd pitch and, after three pitons, noticed a mantel-hold. Realizing the route could be free-climbed using that hold, he lowered to where he had started aid-climbing and, seeing no reason to unclip his rope from the three pitons, made the free lead. His style on most climbs was good, but these few routes were at the top of the standard of the day and warranted the scrutiny of his peers. Later climbers were able to recognize the handicaps that in some cases affected his performance. On both routes, he was belayed by a fourteen-year-old Roger Briggs, used a stretchy nylon rope, and carried a heavy rack of pitons and a hammer. He used no chalk. That he did not openly declare the minor flaws in style was more suspect than were the flaws and aroused ire especially among those who were threatened by his advances and inclined to criticize. To answer the doubts in himself, Ament returned to these routes and did each in better style.

Ament free-climbed the classic Super Slab route in Eldorado

in May 1967, taking care to avoid any stylistic flaw, and led Tongo (5.10+ or 5.11-) on Castle Rock in the same year, again exercising good style. In spring of '67, he also led the 5.11 free ascent of Country Club Crack -- one of Boulder's most elegant routes.

Larry Dalke in 1967 free-climbed X-M on the Bastille, a bold series of four 5.10 pitches that exacted essentially unquestionable style due to a shortage of good protection. Although not as difficult as Ament's routes, this was undoubtedly of at least equal significance.

Larry Dalke / photo by Pat Ament

As early as 1965, Ament envisioned free-climbing Eldorado's Naked Edge and was preparing to fulfill his dream in 1967 when a difficult personal experience in his life destroyed for a few years his interest in longer climbs. He maintained an interest, however, in bouldering.

The single hardest moves in rock climbing were, as always, to be found in bouldering. From 1967 to late 1969, no one in the area pursued the activity more intensely than Ament who briefly had competed as a University gymnast and now was a disciple of bouldering master John Gill. Ament bouldered often alone, sometimes wearing his no-friction penny-loafers, or in the company of other boulderers such as Paul Hagan, Richard Smith, Bob Poling, Eric Varney, and Gill. Varney, a beginner, weighed about 90 pounds and discovered he could pull his body up easily by his fingers. Not interested in long climbs, a rare visitor even to bouldering, he worked out the Varney Direct up the center of the Red Wall Boulder. It was a difficult problem facilitated by his lightness -- Varney admitted wryly. In the late '60s, Gill made several visits to Flagstaff Mountain and put up one route of particular note -- the Gill Swing, an amazing aerial leap to a sloping hold (on the overhang a few inches right of Richard Smith's famous overhang). Gill and Ament, both gymnasts, were the first to use chalk for bouldering. Ament had been the first to use it on actual rock climbs, carrying a small block in a pocket or in his mouth (since chalk bags did not yet exist). One of Ament's boulder routes (not his hardest), ascended the Right Side Of The Red Wall. Over twenty years later, this route would be included in several articles and a book listing important bouldering problems in America. In the early 1970's, the route became the frustration of Bob Williams who at last, using Duco cement, tried gluing the fingertips of his left hand onto the first hold! He was caught in the act by Steve Wunsch who happened by. Williams, known for his susceptibility to tearing off the soft pads of his fingers, had impressively springy legs and strong arms and put up Double-Clutch -- a dynamic lunge of substantial difficulty up the northwest overhang of Beer Barrel Rock.

Pat Ament with block of chalk in mouth (before chalk bags) boulders on Flagstaff in the 1960's

Having set aside his dream of the Naked Edge, Ament encouraged Wisconsin climber and now Boulder resident Jim Erickson to try the route. Erickson already had led several impressive free ascents, such as Rincon and Grandmother's Challenge and accepted the invitation. The route became Jim's obsession. He attempted it a number of times, and the first pitch was led free in 1971 by his partner Steve Wunsch. Later in '71, Erickson and Duncan Ferguson free-climbed the entire route. Ament greeted them on top, making a short super-8 film looking down at them on the last pitch. This route, with three 5.11 pitches, was the high point of many excellent free ascents done by Erickson during the '70s. His 1973 free ascents of Scotch 'N Soda and Dead On Arrival -- 5.11b -- in Eldorado were to have harder single moves but would fall short of the grandeur of the Edge. In '72, Roger Briggs and Erickson free-climbed the towering wall of Diving Board in Eldorado. Ferguson in 1972, with Don Peterson, free-climbed the Bastille's Wide Country. Roger Briggs led his infamous, overhanging crack auspiciously named Death And Transfiguration, on the north wall of the Fourth Flatiron, another achievement to distinguish the year 1972. Bob Williams, who preferred bouldering, pulled off the free ascent of the C'est La Vie dihedral in 1973, one of Eldorado's most difficult -- although most well-protected -- 5.11 routes. Henry Barber, also in '73, flashed Vertigo Direct -- a sensational finish up the overhang above Eldorado's Vertigo dihedral. Among Barber's feats was a free-solo of Gorilla's Delight on the Dome in Boulder Canyon. He had been lured onto the climb by inaccurate information about its grade and, thinking it moderate, found himself committed on 5.10- rock.

Jim Erickson leading Grandmother's Challenge / photo by Bob Godfrey --

By now Kor and Dalke each had married and, having joined the same religion, climbed rarely if at all. The number of serious rock climbers had increased, from two dozen or so in the early 1960's to several thousand. No more was there a sense of a small, secret culture, and the new climbers were deliberate in their intentions of free climbing routes done originally with aid. Some individuals who had done aid ascents in the '60s returned to make free ascents of their own routes, a simple change of focus.

Throughout the years, a number of women expressed a majestic level of rock climbing ability, such as Ma Greenman, Judy Rearick, and Jane Bendixen, but none more so than ballet dancer Diana Hunter who in 1973 humbled her male companions with sight-leads of such testpieces as the first pitch of Wide Country (5.10+) and the crux of the Bastille's Northwest Corner (5.10+ or 5.11-). Diana had the idea one day of making a salad using poison-ivy leaves. She had heard that eating a bit of the dreaded plant would allow her to build up an immunity to it. She suffered a severe systemic reaction (a rash covering her entire body).

Other women to emerge as talented individuals of climbing were Molly Higgins, Jean Ruwitch, Coral Bowman, and -- the eventual most brilliant and prolific female star of Boulder climbing -- Beth Bennet. Destined to participate in the first female ascents of the Naked Edge and Jules Verne, Beth's accomplishments also included difficult bouldering.

Beth Bennet on Flagstaff

An important name among free-climbers during the 1970's continued to be the socially very quiet, almost reclusive, Duncan Ferguson. Naturally talented, in the manner of Larry Dalke, Duncan championed difficult ascents, including a 1974, on-sight, unprotected wall called the Uplift in Eldorado (5.10+).

There were others ways in which climbers excelled through the years. For example, Bob Culp and Gary Neptune ran successful climbing shops. Neptune -- another Boulder climber destined to succeed at Everest -- got some of his initial exposure when he "streaked" the Third Flatiron (went up naked). Pat Ament authored John Gill's biography and, by way of Gill, introduced the climbing world to a higher mentality. As a climbing mentor, in the example of his own inspirations (Rearick, and Robbins), Ament influenced a number of individual stars, including Roger Briggs, Christian Griffith, Dan Stone, and Eric Doub.

Baker Armstrong at age 60 climbed the east face of the Third in 16 minutes.

Baker Armstrong

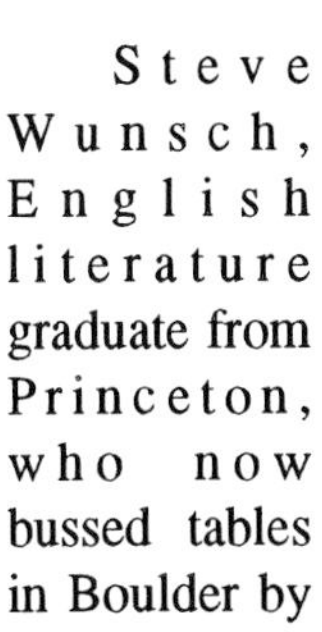

Steve Wunsch, English literature graduate from Princeton, who now bussed tables in Boulder by night and climbed by day, led the 4th pitch of Jules Verne free in Eldorado in 1975, a striking, exquisite, aesthetic, vertical pitch, without much protection at its crux. Bill Putnam had led the first pitch of the route free in 1972, and Erickson and Ferguson had attempted the route in '73. The day before Wunsch made the lead, he managed to place two dubious, small, wire nuts and got past the crux but then, to the astonishment of onlookers, down-climbed the difficult, complex moves. This pitch excited the imagination and fear of area climbers and the disappointment of David Breashears who had set his sights on it.

David Breashears

Almost as though needing a greater challenge to replace the idea of Jules Verne, Breashears (with Steve Mammen) in 1975 went to the Mickey Mouse (Red Dihedral Wall) above Eldorado and led Perilous Journey and Krystal Klyr. These two short routes had no protection at all (except a single, questionable point halfway up Krystal Klyr) and were 5.11a. Done on-sight, these two routes were more momentous than Jules Verne or even the free ascent of the Naked Edge in 1971 by Erickson and Ferguson -- although the Naked Edge retains its classic, formidable status as the most arresting climb in Eldorado. Sometimes called "the kid," or the Kloeberdanz Kid, Breashears got this name after an on-sight, static lead of the Kloeberdanz roof. Ambling up the talus, he offered a suggestion to Roger Briggs who was working at the Kloeberdanz roof. Briggs answered, "Maybe you'd like to come up here and try it." Breashears did so. After trying the roof Wunsch's original dynamic way, the kid flowed smoothly over without any quick reaches or leaps. Also in the mid-'70s, Breashears led free up the Old Bad Aid Crack, something no one had done before, a climb in the mid-5.11 range. His prowess was exhibited on many Eldorado climbs, among which were his 1975 free ascent of Love Minus Zero (5.11) with Art Higbee and John Ruger and his 1975 first continuous free ascent of Side Wall.

In 1975, Steve Wunsch spent many hours working out the free ascent of Eldorado's Psycho roof. Although well protected, the route broke a new barrier of difficulty in Eldorado. Wunsch applied his yoga and honed bouldering skills to create the first route of a 5.12 grade on Eldorado rock. His many attempts at routes were the subject of controversy. He defended the approach and believed in frequent tries. This was his bouldering mentality -- a precursor to sport-climbing which was to appear on the scene within a few years with wide popularity. Erickson, on the other hand, not a good boulderer, found that he excelled at several-pitch climbs, especially those demanding forearm endurance. Erickson defined for himself a "pure" ethic, promoting chalkless ascents without bolts or falls. If one grabbed a carabiner or fell, they failed on the route permanently, in his definition, and could not return to it with the expectation of a free ascent. In a typically jovial moment, Erickson suggested that nude soloing was, logically, the best style. "Taints," as Erickson called stylistic flaws (the term originated with Art Higbee), destroyed the purity of an ascent. Yet his philosophy did not carry altogether in his own experience, as he placed a number of bolts (Hair City, for example). He fell often, including a 30-foot solo fall off the north side of the Fourth Flatiron in 1973 where he broke both legs and a wrist and might have died but for the presence of a hiker. He took a long flyer making the free ascent of Black Walk in Eldorado but, in his climbing guidebook, *Rocky Heights*, made only the minor admission, "...after one attempt." Ament, perhaps more saftey conscious, viewed a fall as the more dubious of styles -- unless a fall was controlled, off a boulder or on a route with protection nearby. Ament made it his own ethic never to fall, whereas Erickson liked falling. Erickson sometimes used his lack of chalk to justify a failure, saying, "If I'd have had chalk, I could have done it." Ament, almost in parody, never could get enough chalk, using it as would a gymnast, to ready his mind, sometimes standing grievously long on a stance to enjoy the feel of the white powder on his fingers. They were good friends, and climbed together often, but had their differences of opinion.

Tom Higgins, a California climber who was a stylistic perfectionist, actually lived Erickson's ethic. Visiting Eldorado in 1975, Higgins started up the Naked Edge with his friend Bob Kamps. As Higgins followed the first pitch, having little difficulty, his foot popped off a small edge. A few pounds of his body weight came onto the rope, and he elected to retreat from the climb -- having lost the chance of doing the route in perfect style.

The Naked Edge was free-soloed in the later-'70s by Jim Collins, an astounding achievement -- with three 5.11 pitches and one 5.10 (and these were not crack pitches where a body might wedge and find security, rather openly exposed moves over gaping drops). He had done the route many times and, he said, "wired it." Although in his best shape ever, Jim admitted he brought along a sling and two carabiners in case he got scared and needed them.

Eldorado's second route of a 5.12 grade, in 1976, happened more easily than Psycho, when strong Greg Lowe ascended out under the overhang of Clever Lever. Also in '76, Roger Briggs (with Scott Woodruff) pioneered Lene's Dream (5.11), a bold free-climb straight up the blank-looking wall above the crux of Jules Verne.

In 1977, Steve Wunsch and Kevin Bein free-climbed the West Overhang of the Maiden, a task with formidable exposure, and California's John Bachar in 1978 put together the free ascent of Eldorado's outlandishly overhanging Wisdom. Gymnast Bob Candelaria had previously gotten out to the lip of the Wisdom roof but took a huge, falling swing through space when a flake broke off in his hand. Candelaria, an excellent boulderer, did many difficult free-climbs -- the most controversial of which was his free ascent in the mid-later '70s of Papillion, a 5.12 right-angling crack up the exposed, top north wall of the Third Flatiron. Two excellent climbers who later attempted to repeat this reported an abundance of lichen and no sign of chalk. They could not believe it had been climbed. People tended to doubt Candelaria's honesty until they saw him climb or tried to climb with him. He was capable of much, although his credibility was weakened a small bit when he re-located a bolt more strategically on the route X-M -- a route that had required climbers to face their fear. The bolt was later removed, an expression of a growing schism between "traditionalists" and a new "sport-climbing" generation eager to have a more ready use of bolts. Candelaria in 1978 led the bold Vertigo Direct Start in Eldorado, another huge overhang, estimated to be 5.12.

Jim Collins free-climbed Genesis in Eldorado in 1979, taking something like 50 falls over many days to work out the 5.12c crux. This type of bouldering "high up" reflected the lust of new climber's for new challenges. Meanwhile, of course, the world of bouldering continued to exist, as always, somewhat apart from the world of longer rock climbs. Six-foot-four Jim Holloway especially became known as a marvel of bouldering and was referred to by John Gill as "the fabulous Holloway." The highest standard ever was achieved on Flagstaff by Holloway whose routes seemed to out reach those people they did not simply out class.

Jim Holloway on Flagstaff Mountain, photo by Pat Ament

From the later 1970's through the mid-'80s, the three bright stars of Flagstaff bouldering in addition to Holloway were Bob Candelaria, Jim Michael, and Christian Griffith.

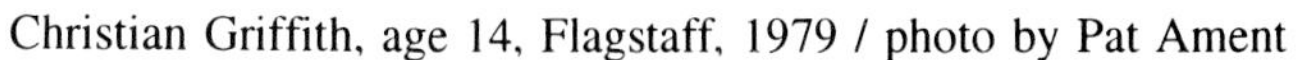

Christian Griffith, age 14, Flagstaff, 1979 / photo by Pat Ament

Jim Michael had honed his remarkable bouldering skill as Holloway's favorite partner and climbed, it seemed, most places the much taller Holloway went. Candelaria's gymnastic prowess was demonstrated one day on Flagstaff when he managed Pratt's mantel and then pressed into a handstand on it.

A climber of obvious talent, Charlie Fowler, in 1979 led N.E.D. -- a 5.12 roof looming above the cement platform at the southwest corner of Eldorado's Whale's Tail.

English climbing star Alec Sharp made Boulder his home in 1977 and in '79 demonstrated his superb talent as a free-climber, pioneering many difficult routes -- such as Never A Dull Moment, on Castle Rock, a 5.11+ vertical face followed by a taxing finger-hand/lieback crack. After two falls from the crack and retreating, Sharp returned another day and succeeded -- even with the crack wet after a spell of rain. A few of his styles were questioned by traditionalists, including the blatant use of a long house ladder in Boulder Canyon to place a bolt on a route. People wondered what climbing was coming to. No one, however, questioned Alec's ability as a climber or the quality of his person.

By now, state-of-the-art, sticky rubber shoes (the first were called "Fire," pronounced fee-ray) made climbing much easier and contributed to escalating standards. Cracks were easily protected with "Friends" (camming devices), and climbers trained with the fervor of Olympians. The number of climbers, as well as new routes, magnified almost to infinity.

Roger Briggs, now a trained runner with tremendous leg power and endurance, in 1980 free-climbed Higher Wisdom (also called Scary Canary), a route approaching 5.12 in difficulty and ascending a menacing, terrifying, overhanging dihedral above the Wisdom roof. Jim Erickson showed that he was not yet over the hill, joining forces with Briggs and leading the overhanging crack of Super Power in Skunk Canyon. Erickson felt that this was one of his best climbs. While he would remember the much longer Naked Edge for "its insight, spiritual development, and perseverance," this route was more important to him in terms of pure achievement.

In 1980, Jeff Achey led Wendego, a 5.12 free ascent of an aid-climb located on the beautiful Rincon Wall in the upper west end of Eldorado. The next year, in Eldorado, Jeff free-climbed Le Void (5.11+) with Roger Briggs and, in Boulder Canyon, free climbed all but the crux start of Tourist Extravagance. Skip Guerin and Bob Horan in 1981 put up the overhanging Blues Power (5.12a), an overhanging hand-crack on Eldorado's West Ridge. The North Face of Seal Rock (5.11+), done free in 1982 by Jeff Achey and Roger Briggs, and Doric Dihedral (5.12), led free in 1983 by Chip Ruckgaber, were illustrations of skill and boldness during the early '80s.

While bolt-happy, lycra tights-clad sport-climbers rappelled from the top and the fashions of a new generation began to assert themselves, others continued to use whatever means they could to avoid bolts. In 1981, Jeff Achey did two routes on the Mickey Mouse where he employed bolt-avoiding methods. Beginner's Mind required that a climber "Bring a number 4 crack 'n up and be prepared to fall on it!" On Scorpius, Jeff mentioned that "Thin pitons were hand-placed for protection!" Pat Adams, one of the more lean and strong climbers of the 1980's, free-soloed the Kloeberdanz roof in Eldorado, using a finger-hold that broke off in the hands of Pat Ament who did the route (belayed) days later.

Derek Hersey, another English climber who located in Boulder, was suited to soloing. With his relaxed, carefree temperament, he made the second free-solo of the Naked Edge in 1984 and made many other solo ascents during the '80s. Bob Horan, who led Eldorado's Rainbow Wall free in 1984, was a prime mover among '80s free-climbers. He free-soloed Eldorado's N.E.D. (5.12) an inspired (or deranged?) moment in the mid-'80s.

Christian Griffith, unwilling to embrace the ethical concerns of traditional climbers, advocated rappel-bolted sport-climbs. Among his exploits was a 5.12+ first free ascent in 1985 of the Red Dihedral (on the Mickey Mouse) with Eric Doub. In case anyone thought that sport-climbing was altogether safe, Christian took a forty-foot fall off the Red Dihedral, while rushing, late in the day, attempting to clip a piece of protection on the 2nd pitch of the dihedral. He pulled one of Kor's aging bolts -- which he brought home to hang on his wall. That epic day had started with his solo of Breashears' Perilous Journey. Also this year (1985), Christian free climbed Castle Rock's Tourist Extravagance (perhaps the first 5.13 in the area). After first top-roping and pre-bolting, he climbed Paris Girl (5.12+). A bolt war resulted, with the bolts of Paris Girl being chopped and then replaced.

Christian did the 5.12c first ascent of Verve (a futuristic, overhanging arete in Boulder Canyon), Je T'aime (a vertical slab in

Eldorado), Wingless Victory (a 5.13b bolted route on the airy prow right of the 4th pitch of the Naked Edge), and the 5.13c, spectacularly exposed, giant overhang of Desdichado, all in 1986. Desdichado was, perhaps, the most difficult sport-climb in the country at that time.

Reacting to the chopping of Paris Girl, Christian offered his "manifesto," a written summary of his attitudes, stating, "The slaughter of the last bastions of traditionalism has begun." This "slaughter," or rather rape (as some saw it), was to be carried out by those Christian called "the new power that will decide what direction climbing should go." He believed that the danger/adventure aspect needed to be diminished for the sake of the gymnastic/bouldering aspect of the future. It was, as he saw it, the responsibility of a new generation to define itself and that they deserved the space to do so. Christian later would tone down his rhetoric, as the level of his maturity grew slightly and upon starting a company of his own called Verve -- where he designed chalkbags, tights, and other equipment for climbers.

Charlie Fowler one day in '86 observed, "Christian is just getting so good that it is becoming harder and harder for him to find rock difficult enough to express his talents." Christian in 1987 squeezed out the route Lakme (5.13b) on the sheer arete between Genesis and Desdichado. He and Dale Goddard were the standard bearers of a new, superbly trained generation of sport-climbers eager and able to make their own rules and push standards. Among these individuals was Chris Hill who engineered the first free ascent of the Web (a 5.13 up the overhanging quartzite wall left of Supremacy Crack). Goddard, light and strong, pioneered difficult sport-climbs in the mid-'80s -- such as Cornucopia (a 5.13a route in '86 on Dinosaur Mountain) and The Sacred And The Profane (a 5.12d or 5.13a route on Eldorado's Peanuts Wall).

Throughout the '80s, the brightest light among traditionalist climbers was, undoubtedly, Derek Hersey who -- to everyone's awe -- free-soloed Eldorado routes such as Vertigo, the Naked Edge, and Northwest Corner of the Bastille. Several times, he soloed Black Walk and then solo down-climbed Back Talk. He pioneered a difficult (5.11+ or 5.12-), mostly unprotected line left of the prominent prow (or arete) below Super Slab and named it "To R. P. Or Not To Be." The name was a play on a 5.14, bolted sport route on Oregon's Smith Rock, called "To Bolt Or Not To Be."

A 1985 issue of *Outside Magazine* referred to the vertical

and seemingly holdless right side (south wall) of the Milton Boulder in Eldorado as "Colorado's great unclimbed problem." *Outside*, in its ridiculous pursuit of the latest hype, catered to the sensational and to the growing numbers of climbers. Six-foot-seven Oklahoman Jimmy Ratzlaff, a basketball player, ran at the wall and leaped -- managing to grab the top. He named the feat Nothing's Impossible. In 1986, unaware of Ratzlaff's jump-ascent, Steve Mammen climbed the wall in more conventional style. He worked on the problem for six weeks. In *Stone Crusade, A Historical Guide To Bouldering In America*, author John Sherman describes the Mammen ascent, "...he finally managed an absurd, half-blind double dyno off the ground (one hand lunges for an inverted layaway, while the opposite foot kicks for a nickel edge). He then linked it with the tenuous twin sloper thumb underclings above." Let's just say it was hard. This route was indication of continued pursuit of bouldering by high level stars -- there were many during the '80s, not the least of whom were Bob Horan, Skip Guerin, John Sherman, and Chris Jones. Certainly there were many thousand "last great unclimbed problems" yet among the Boulder rocks.

A 5.12 first ascent led by a woman occurred in 1987 when Andrea Azoff put up the runout sport-route Just Another Girl's Climb with Charlie Fowler. Lynn Hill, America's best female climber, visited Eldorado and, belayed by Ament, used only two points of protection to sight-lead Supremacy Crack.

Much of climbing throughout the country was becoming by now a commercial venture. Magazines seemed to favor sport-climbing, and climbing competitions were frequent. Sponsorship by commercial entities was a commodity climbers fought for. Climbers sought jobs, support, or simply free equipment, putting together climbing resumes for the purpose of listing their recognition and accomplishments. Jim Karn and Robyn Erbesfield would establish themselves as two of Boulder's and the world's top professional climbers. Others to become excellent competition climbers included Pat Adams, Bobbie Bensman, Dan Michael, Will Gad, and Steve Hong. In Eldorado, Karn led (in "red-point" style) White Lies -- a 5.13 direct finish out the upper roof of Kloeberdanz, in 1988. The name of the route reflected his suspicion that Bob Candelaria, the author of the line in 1987, had not done the route without cheats.

The first use of a Bosch power drill occurred in 1988 when Colin Lantz, a brilliant new talent, created the overhanging route Your Mother on the high, southwest end of the Bastille. Christian

Griffith hand-drilled his bolts, as did other climbers. The notion of quickly placed bolts captured the imagination of sport-climbers and opened the way for casual bolting. Bolts went in... unnecessarily by the less able who simply hoped to follow the example (or rather take advantage) of the new fad.

A number of outstanding climbers from England and Europe visited the Boulder area and Eldorado. France's Patrick Edlinger in 1988 top-roped Bob Horan's sport-climb Beware Of The Future, on the arete left of Doric Dihedral (in Skunk Canyon), rating the route (after a key hold broke) 5.13d or 5.14a. England's Gerry Moffat climbed many Eldorado routes and demonstrated bouldering skill to match his jocund impertinence. England's Ben Moon in 1991 free-climbed Eldorado's Temporary Like Achilles, an imposing roof Christian had established new bolts for but not yet succeeded at. Moon also made the second ascent of Jim Holloway's difficult boulder problem, A.H.R., although via a slightly easier variation.

In 1990, Colin Lantz led The Violator, 5.13c, in Fern Canyon, and Rock Atrocity, 5.13d, on Dinosaur Mountain, then in 1991 led Honemaster Lambada, 5.13d, on the backside of the Ironing Boards. These sport-climbs, controversial for their bolts yet archetypes of the new standards, were among the last to be done with rappel-placed bolts, since -- after heated public debates -- bolting finally was banned in the Boulder area by park and city officials. Christian Griffith later reflected that climber problems with these officials might not have existed had it not been for Bosch drills and the radical increase in bolting that took place among the flatiron areas. Although Christian was willing to rappel to pre-place bolts, he never had used a power drill. Even on rappel, it was difficult with a hand-held drill to place a bolt -- a difficulty that, in Christian's opinion, naturally limited the amount of bolts used. "On Desdichado," he noted, "I used four bolts, not ten."

A few individuals among the most exceptional of the new climbers began in the early and mid-1990's to reveal a desire to return to their stylistic roots. For example, a sub-culture of modern traditionalists repeated some of the old, scary routes and made free ascents of a high standard without rappel-placed bolts. Peter Croft, one of Yosemite's (and America's) great new stars, honored Supremacy Crack with an on-sight free-solo.

June 4, 1993, a foggy, English afternoon in Eldorado, climbers of all ages and philosophies gathered in the gentle park beside the river at the west end of the canyon to share their thoughts about Derek Hersey who was killed when he fell while soloing in Yosemite. A few days after this commemoration, his ashes were scattered to the four winds from the sunset-lit summit of the Yellow Spur.

Derek Hersey, Eldorado, early 1990's / photo by Pat Ament

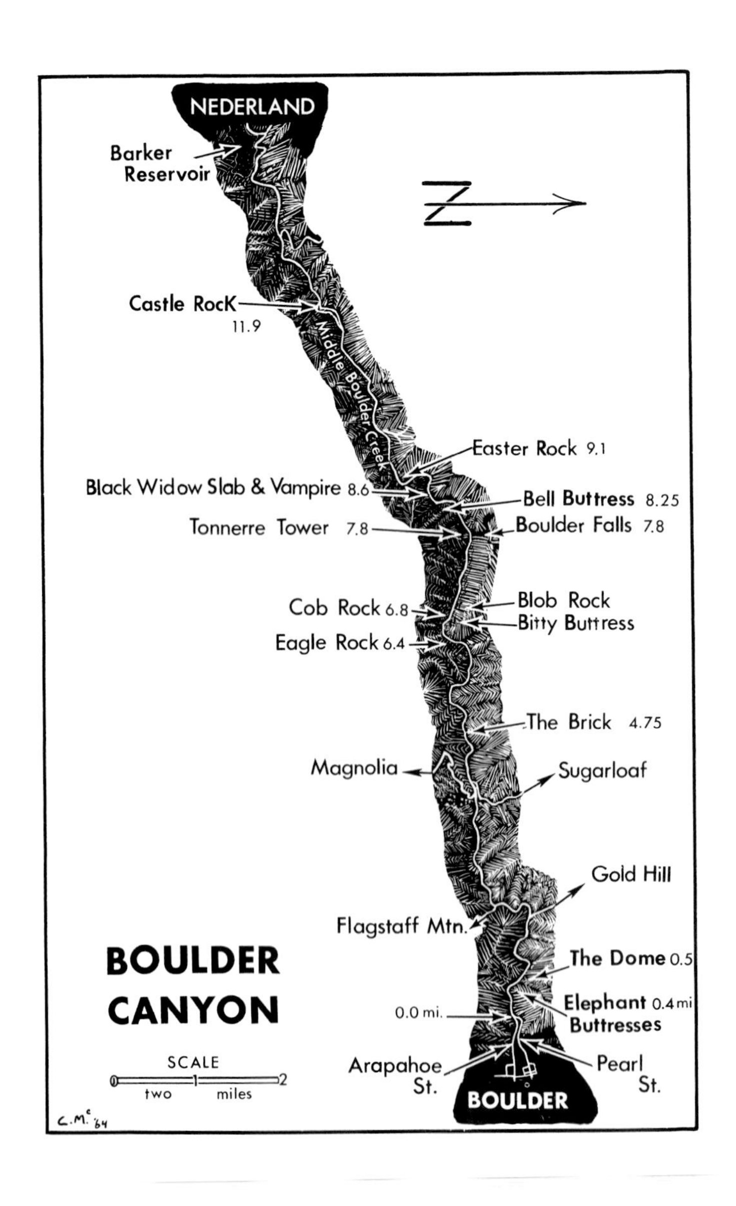
NEDERLAND
Barker Reservoir
N
Castle RocK 11.9
Middle Boulder Creek
Easter Rock 9.1
Black Widow Slab & Vampire 8.6
Bell Buttress 8.25
Tonnerre Tower 7.8
Boulder Falls 7.8
Cob Rock 6.8
Blob Rock
Bitty Buttress
Eagle Rock 6.4
The Brick 4.75
Magnolia
Sugarloaf
Gold Hill
Flagstaff Mtn.
BOULDER CANYON
The Dome 0.5
Elephant 0.4 mi Buttresses
0.0 mi.
SCALE
0 1 2
two miles
Arapahoe St.
Pearl St.
BOULDER
C.M. '64

BOULDER CANYON

About twelve miles of canyon abundant with granite close to the road can be reached by a short drive or bike ride west up Canyon Boulevard from central Boulder. Climbing has had a long tradition in this canyon, beginning with those first to scale the Dome and Castle Rock. Perhaps early miners found ways up some of the rocks. Boulder Falls has long been a tourist attraction, inviting the unskilled to attempt climbing. The rock in the Boulder Falls area tends to be wet and hidden much of the time from sun, making it rotten and dangerous. The nature of Boulder Canyon rock is different than that of Eldorado, with large blocks that must be avoided or bypassed with care. While the best routes are reasonably free of loose rock, a climber must always be on the alert.

Elephant Buttresses

These are the four blocky, broken towers near the road, on the northeast side of the river, about .05 mile up Boulder Canyon. The buttresses are numbered from north to south (hence the 4th Buttress is the largest rock and southernmost). Crossing the river is sometimes possible via boulder hopping, but never underestimate the swiftness or strength of the river. A bridge now exists a short distance west (up river) after which a trail can be found leading east to the buttresses. Beware of poison ivy along the approach during the spring and summer.

There are countless routes on these rocks, some of which will speak to you individually, for example the nice, short, easy climb up to the tree on the 2nd Elephant Buttress (just left of the gully that divides the 2nd Buttress from the 3rd). **Monster Woman** goes over a roof a short distance above the water pipe near the middle of the 3rd Elephant Buttress. The logical, meandering route up the west face of the 3rd Buttress is also popular.

Tough Situation. 5.9+. First free ascent in 1972 by Duncan Ferguson and Jim Erickson. This is the short, left-facing dihedral on the northwest side of the upper block of the 2nd Elephant Buttress. Scramble up easy rock, via a gully, to a big ledge at the start of the dihedral. The crux is the initial overhang in the dihedral, although the dihedral above requires tricky, strenuous finger/hand-jamming. The possibilities for nut protection are excellent. The beauty of this minor route is how it forces from a climber precise technique and leads the climber through a series of interesting moves. Without good footwork, the arms tire quickly.

Classic Finger-Crack. 5.9. First known free ascent in the 1960's led by Pat Ament. This is a thin, beautiful crack piercing a flat, steep wall high on the southwest facing summit block of the 2nd Elephant Buttress. Excellent, small-nut placements allow for a well-protected, elegant short climb that requires careful footwork to prevent over-exertion of the fingers and arms.

F-M. 5.11c or d, possibly 5.12a for shorter people. And aid-climb of unknown origin, first led free in 1974 by Roger Briggs. This masterpiece of climbing is one of the finest in Boulder Canyon. Excellent (although strenuous to place) protection allows for a safe, slightly overhanging, creatively challenging ascent. The route goes up the steepest northwest wall of the 3rd Elephant Buttress, via a horrendous-looking, left-facing dihedral. The dihedral can be reached by traversing along a ledge south into it from a gully or by a steep, 5.10 pitch directly up a wall with a finger/hand-crack. Stem rests are available for people with long legs, but otherwise a leader must burn energy to conserve energy while ascending the overhanging portion of the dihedral. As the overhang subsides, an easier dihedral leads to a ledge.

West Face of 4th Elephant Buttress. 5.8+. Old piton remnants and scars indicate early aid ascents, but a lovely (and steep) free-climb is found here up the west face of the 4th Buttress. The route can be seen as a crack that diagonals upward and slightly left, approximately in the center of the west face. Either start at the lowest point of the wall and begin angling upward slightly to the left on rock that seems not as good quality as usual or make the preferred traverse to the crack, starting from the south end of the water pipe. This traverse begins with a tricky balance move, and it is wise to set a piece of protection after the move in order to protect the second person. It is not a bad idea to belay on a small stance at the end of the traverse, at the start of the crack that angles up the west face. Otherwise, rope drag may develop. With care, the entire route can be done in one long pitch.

To descend from the summit, scramble and walk down the east side of the rock to the east entrance of the water tunnel. Continue downward and come around the south side of the rock, or -- if there is no water in the tunnel -- sneak through the bat-inhabited tunnel. On a hot day, it is fun to take off shoes and wade through the tunnel back to the start.

The Dome

This granite formation sits on the hill above and north of the Elephant Buttresses, .05 mile up Boulder Canyon. Yosemite-like, white, warm granite, southerly exposure, make for a friendly climbing setting. The descent off the rock is easiest to the east.

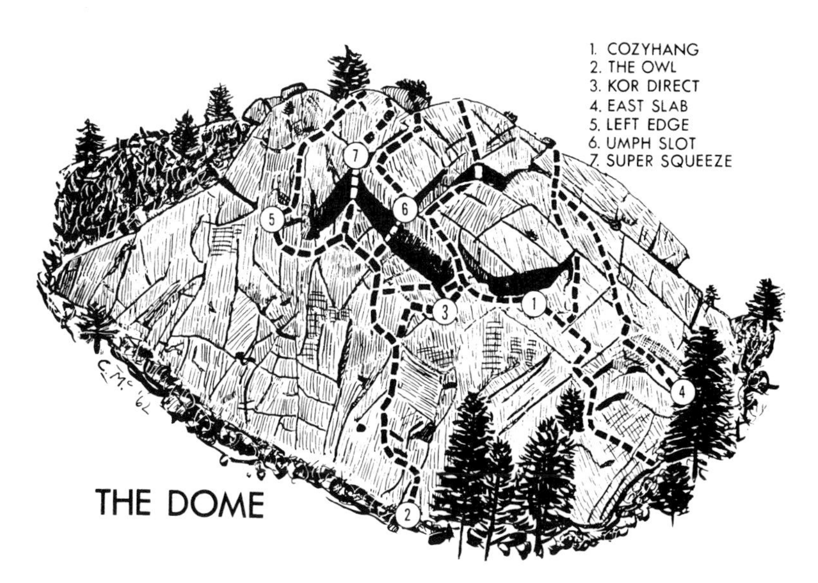

East Slab. 5.5 or 5.6. This is a crack that pierces a smooth, conspicuous slab on the right side of the south face. The route begins approximately 100 feet up the talus east from the lowest point of the rock. Climb an inside-corner, bypass an overhang on the left (or the right, or straight over), and reach a stance at the actual base of the beautiful slab. The 2nd lead goes straight up the slab, with an exciting moment where the crack ends and bare rock remains. Above, pass an overhang with a big step to the right (up onto a foothold).

Cozyhang. 5.7 or 5.8. First ascent in 1953 by Mike O'Brien and Jim Crandle. This classic ascent is generally accomplished in five short leads, enabling the climbers to communicate over the noise of the river. The route begins a short distance (perhaps 75 feet) up to the east from the lowest point of the rock. Scramble diagonally left on a slab with left-angling cracks. At the end of the cracks, three small overhangs confront the climber. The highest and largest overhang is virtually the crux of the climb, surmounted near a crack that angles left through the overhang. A less difficult variation is a delicate move around the overhang to the left and then a slab move to the ledge above. The next pitch climbs up and slightly left, first on the easy slab and then making a few balance moves left to a belay stance under the large, obvious roof. From here, the route takes a blind lead to the left (west), below the ceiling. A climber is forced to crouch tightly, in a kind of squatting position, beneath the roof, while reaching around a corner left to feel for a hold that is sometimes wet. This traverse can also be done lower, with hands where the feet are in the first variation. In either case, reach a sloping belay shelf around the corner. From the shelf, step left and work up a hand-crack (or climb directly above the shelf) to a good ledge. From here, traverse easily 40 feet or so diagonally up and right (east) to a stance under a large, A-shaped overhang. The final pitch ascends this awkward overhang and up a simple hand-jam to the top.

The Umph Slot. 5.11 (much easier for thinner people and lizards). First ascent in 1964 with one point of aid by Pat Ament and Wayne Goss. Led free in 1965 by Chuck Pratt. This is a tight slot that breaks a large overhang half way up the left side of the Dome. It was led free by perhaps the best off-width climber of all time. The route strangely is as difficult to aid as to free-climb. There is no easy way up, but a classic, elegant, off-width is the challenge.

Gorilla's Delight. 5.10a. First ascent in 1965 by Pat Ament and George Hurley. Ament led the first dihedral (5.9+), then worked left an easy way to the top (not having the right protection to lead his first idea which was a thin seam above the initial dihedral). Following the pitch, Hurley moved right and created the popular finish -- a steep finger/hand-crack. The route was free-soloed in the 1970's by Henry Barber. Start left of a huge A-shaped overhang (the overhang is **Super Squeeze**, a 5.10+ route led free in the mid-'60s by Pat Ament). At the lower-left edge of the A-shaped overhang is a vertical, left-facing dihedral that ends after a short distance on a high-angle slab. At the top of the dihedral, move right, on the slab, to a flake/crack that is the tricky finale to this brief, excellent route.

The Brick Wall

This classic, south-facing wall, a popular top-roping area, is located 4.6 miles up Boulder Canyon on the north side of the road. Smooth, nearly vertical, but only half a rope length high, it provides several good top-rope routes. A number of difficult climbs have also been done as roped leads or been free-soloed. Layton Kor top-roped a 5.10 route in 1963 that started up the right side of the face, along a left-slanting crack, traversed left across the mid-level sloping ledge to the left corner of the face, and then continued steeply to the top.

Established Variation. 5.10d. Normally done as a top-rope but first done as a roped (mostly unprotected) lead in 1971 by Duncan Ferguson. This beautiful classic starts by ascending the right margin of the wall via a line of small, good holds just left of the left-slanting crack. A delicate move standing up on a small foothold achieves a sloping ledge. Traverse left along the narrow sloping ledge a few feet to a steeper wall with two parallel, vertical finger-cracks. The route climbs somewhat between the two cracks, occasionally with hands in one or the other crack. The crux is suddenly encountered, getting to and getting past a sloping, slippery, horizontal crack.

Crease. 5.11a or b. First known ascent in 1976, top-roped, by Pat Ament. Perhaps the most elegant top-rope on the wall, this more or less follows a thin, obscure line just left of a small crease and up the steep center of the wall. This line joins the Established Variation at the sloping ledge half way up.

The Perfect Route. 5.10b. First ascent in 1970 by Pat Ament and Jim Erickson. The 1st pitch cannot be protected other than by spot and is a steep, short wall with a black streak on the bottom, left side of the rock. This first section was done as a boulder problem as far back as 1964 by Royal Robbins, Pat Ament, and others. Climb over a small lip at the bottom of the wall, then step left to the black streak. Ascend the black streak unprotected, reach an overhang, move left onto a shelf, and climb the bulge above the right end of the shelf (5.9, scary) to a large belay ledge. Above, work up into a left-slanting dihedral that is thin and tricky but well protected. At the top of the dihedral, either move left on easy rock or finish with Bob Candelaria's 1973 "High Exposure Exit" -- a terrifying-looking but actually moderate (5.8+) overhang with a crack leading up and right, through the overhang.

Cob Rock

Located 6.6 miles up Boulder Canyon on the left (south), the north face has a distinguishing inside-corner that becomes a diagonal trough slanting left (east). Many excellent climbs are found here, when the river is low enough to permit access.

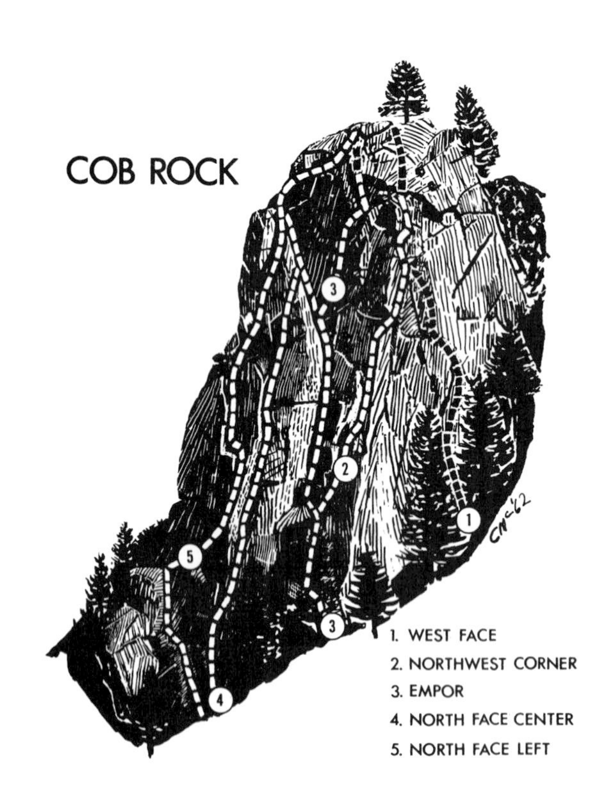

Huston Crack. 5.8+. First ascent in the early 1950's by Cary Huston. This 50 or 60-foot, steep crack is located almost at the lowest northeast corner of Cob Rock. Everything from hand-jams to fists, to off-width technique is required.

Empor. 5.7+. First ascent in 1954 by George Lamb and Dallas Jackson. At one time, this route was considered one of the more formidable free-climbs in the area. The route follows the most obvious line on the rock, starting atop a huge talus boulder near the northwest corner of Cob. The boulder itself is a challenge, offering several possibilities -- including a chimney, a slab, or the west side of the boulder on small holds finishing with a mantel. From the top of the boulder, climb steep, tricky rock approximately 40 feet to a shelf. Move up and left toward the obvious right-facing dihedral (inside-corner). Follow the dihedral and continue up it as it becomes the big trough. After about 25 feet, belay in the trough or at a stance along its outer edge. Make a delicate traverse a few feet diagonally right, to a precarious stance at the base of a crack. With an open-palm jam with the right hand, begin the final moves toward the top.

North Face Center. 5.7. First ascent in 1959 by Layton Kor and George Hurley. Climb the right-facing, inside-corner/crack system near the center of the face (and left/east of the large, obvious inside-corner). Arrive at the large, slanting trough of Empor.

East Edge. 5.10a. First ascent in 1962 by Pat Ament and Larry Dalke. Led free in 1966 by Larry Dalke. This is an excellent route up the left (east) side of the north face of Cob. A thin crack is seen a short distance right (west) of the northwest edge of the rock. This thin crack is the route and involves delicate free-climbing with good protection. Scramble up to a ledge below the actual smooth wall. Climb a difficult-to-protect, small, left-facing inside-corner to the right side of a potentially loose, downward-hanging block. Carefully bypass this block (a type of small overhang) on its right edge. Above the block, hand-traverse and face-climb upward left to the thin crux crack which is followed to a ledge near a prominent block resting horizontally on the edge of Cob. Move right from the block and follow easier cracks to the obvious trough below the summit. The summit will be found without trouble.

Bitty Buttress

This rock is located high above the road, on the north side of the canyon, directly across the river from Cob Rock. To approach, hike up a steep, rocky, grass-filled gully that drops from below the southeast ridge of the buttress. As always in Boulder Canyon, be careful not to knock rocks onto cars.

Bitty Buttress Route. 5.8+. First ascent in 1964 by Paul Mayrose and Pat Ament. Paul's wife wanted him to name a climb after her. "Yes, Bitty," he replied. This route is the obvious, southeast ridge of the buttress. From just left of a tree, climb right, then straight up smooth slabs over a crux section. Reach a belay stance near a small, slightly rotten inside-corner. Climb 10 feet, work 6 feet right, to the actual ridge, and climb to some ledges. Proceed up a steep crack in a dihedral to a belay stance on a ledge. From here, climb a thin, vertical flake on a steep wall. Eventually traverse left beneath an overhang to a point where the overhang can be surmounted.

Blob Rock.

About 6.6 miles up Boulder Canyon and high above the road to the north is the massive formation of Blob. There are many routes and much adventure to be found. In 1962, Rick Horn and Tex Bossier climbed the **Left Face** (5.8), beginning at the lowest point of the main face and moving up steep gray slabs, then left around an overhanging wall. The remainder of that route followed the obvious, right-angling trough leading up the left side of the rock. Also in 1962, the **Center Direct** was climbed, using some aid, by Deane Moore and Charles Alexander. The crux of this route went through the overhanging wall in the vicinity of a crack near some orange lichen streaks.

Where Eagles Dare. 5.9+. First ascent in 1975 by Scott Woodruff, Dan Hare, and Brad Gilbert. This goes up the center of Blob Rock, a little to the right (east) of center, joining at one point the old Center Direct route at a ledge below a headwall (near the orange lichen streaks mentioned above). Start just right (east) of a large talus boulder. Diagonal left on an easy slab to a right-facing inside-corner. Work up this, then straight over a small overhang and bulging section via a thin crack. Move right, to a belay. Step left and climb a low-angle dihedral with a square roof (poor pro, 5.8+) to a good ledge at the bottom of the obvious, recessed headwall near orange lichen streaks. Climb onto an overhanging flake at the extreme right end of the ledge. Jam over a bulge, move slightly right, ascend a small overhang, and work up to the top via cracks.

Divine Wind. 5.11. First ascent in 1979 by Alec Sharp and Richard Carey. Alec Sharp, English climber turned Boulderite, impressed everyone by pioneering a host of difficult free routes in the later

'70s. This is one of his finest and one of the best (of the more difficult) routes in Boulder Canyon, offering good-quality rock and difficult, creative climbing. The route follows a line of right-facing dihedrals located on the far left (west) side of Blob. To start the 1st pitch, climb a groove, passing the right side of an obvious roof. Climb to an elegant, right-facing dihedral above and proceed up it (small nuts offer protection). At the steepest part of the dihedral, strenuous stemming ends with a step left and less steep rock to a sloping (but good) ledge. Above, a dihedral that looks more like a roof is the final and technical crux (perhaps easier for taller people).

Lower East Block of Blob Rock

A large gully to the right of the center of Blob separates the rock into two parts. The left (west) part is Blob Rock, and the right (southeast part) is the Lower East Block of Blob.

The Crack Tac. 5.9+. First ascent in 1964 by Pat Ament and Fred Pfahler. First free ascent in 1971 by Jim Erickson and Jim Walsh. This lovely, Yosemite-like slab was selected somewhat randomly as a practice aid-climb to test the effectiveness of a new device: Greg Blomberg's "crack tac," a tiny piton similar to a Chouinard R.U.R.P. Cliff hangers (small hooks set on ledges) were used also during the first ascent. Too busy playing with the new gear, the first ascent team did not care if the slab could be free-climbed. In fact the route is an exquisite, one-pitch route full of enjoyable, delicate, slab/face moves. Start near the lower right side of the slab at the bottom southwest side of Blob's Lower East Block. Find a crease (a very shallow crack) that slants upward and slightly right. Beginning here, climb more or less straight up the slab. No bolts were used on the first ascent or on the first free ascent, but later parties added bolts -- at least one of which remains. One can avoid the bolt, to feel the pure sense of adventure. It is worth noting that a much easier start can be found by approaching from the right, but this eliminates some of the most exciting, initial free-climbing. At the end of one rope length, an easy traverse can be found left (north) into the large gully.

A Hike With Ludwig Dude. 5.10a or b. First ascent in 1970 by Bob Poling and Dick Donofrio. This excellent, one-pitch route is as famous for its name as for the enjoyable, challenging, and clean climbing up a steep, granite slab. In the spirit of the Crack Tac, there exists marginal protection. Protection is not altogether absent but requires creativity to find. Start the route directly behind an obvious tree uphill a short distance north from the start of the Crack Tac. The most difficult moves are right off the ground, over a small overhang with a smooth slab above.

Happy Hour Crag

This small, shattered and tipsy-looking cliff is found above the road to the north, obscured somewhat by trees, about 6.7 miles up Boulder Canyon. Near the center of the crag and just east of the route Dementia (described below) is **Cheers**, a rather nice, 5.9+, vertical face-climb with bolts.

Dementia. 5.9+ or 5.10a. First ascent in 1974 or '75 by Chris Scanlon and Dave Rice. The name was given by climbers who made the second ascent. This is the obvious feature of Happy Hour Crag, curving upward in a sheer, inviting way. About 20 feet up, a tricky lieback move (5.8+ or 5.9-, psychologically) and then a short hand-crack lead into the actual Dementia dihedral. Creative stemming, bridging, and footwork, with good protection, end with a step left to an airy foothold. Then squiggle up a kind of hand-crack/slot. Be careful of loose blocks that sit on the top.

Security Risk Crag

This is located high above and right (northeast) of Happy Hour Crag. The cliff is divided into two parts.

Security Risk. 5.10. First ascent in 1978 by Scott Woodruff and Dan Hare. This is located on the right block of Security Risk Crag. Go up an obvious, straight crack after approaching it via an overhanging (left-facing) dihedral and a diagonal finger crack.

Get Smart. 5.10. First ascent in 1981 by Randy Leavitt, Dan Hare, and Joel Schiavone. Near the center of the upper block of Security Risk Crag is a clear crack system to the right of a broken gully. First climb a 5.9, large, right-facing inside-corner to a ledge. Then climb a right-slanting crack through some small roofs. Face climb to a ledge.

Hot Flyer. 5.11+? First ascent in 1981 by Randy Leavitt and Rick Accomazzo. Start roughly 45 feet right of Get Smart, at a ledge. Climb the corners above and left to a rest. Continue to a right-facing inside-corner, then angle up and left over triple roofs. Belay at two bolts above the roofs. Now climb straight up the face (5.9).

Boulder Falls

The granite in this area, 7.5 miles up Boulder Canyon, is in many places hidden from the light and subject to the moist environment of the river and falls. Thus the rock is bad often and somewhat dangerous. A number of accidents have occurred as a result of climbers assuming the rock was solid. Countless routes exist, nevertheless, including far up into the falls canyon. In 1961, Charles Roskosz and Tink Wilson did a route called **Jello** -- a wall on the east side of the creek close to the falls. Bob Culp, in the early '60s, climbed a route near Jello, at one point (thinking he was about to fall) utilizing his parka for support on a rock nubbin. In 1963, Dave Rearick soloed a difficult route in the same area (free, 5.8, for 120 feet).

The Practice Rock

Eight miles up Boulder Canyon, on the north side of the road are two small, smooth, angular blocks on a slab.
Diagonal Crack. 5.11-. This was originally an old, practice aid crack, sometimes done in winter snow. First led free (after top-roping) in 1972 by Bill Putnam. The route is the obvious, left-angling crack across the right block. Start with a steep, vertical crack rather than at the actual beginning of the angling crack.

Bell Buttress

Eight miles up Boulder Canyon, on the south side of the road, is this impressive tower of granite. A descent from the summit of Bell Buttress is one of the toughest challenges and can be made either to the northeast, down tree and talus-covered slopes, or to the south (with possibly a rappel at one point). Approach to Bell Buttress is possible only when the river is low.
Gates Of Eden. 5.10a. First ascent in 1967 by Pat Ament and Danny Smith. This spectacular crack seems to overhang its base. Along the large approach ledge that cuts across the lower part of Bell Buttress, locate a wide chimney (a cavernous gully) that shoots up vertically (actually overhung at its bottom). Immediately left of this wide chimney and on a steep wall is a narrow, overhanging, flared slot that slices upward, beginning as an overhanging hand-jam. From a sloping belay stance above the slot, work upward to the right and into a big dihedral.
Grand Inquisitor. 5.12(?). First ascent in about 1979 or 1980 by Alec Sharp and Chuck Fitch. This is an impressive route up the

overhanging wall just left of Gates of Eden and famous for the reason that a large house ladder was used to place a bolt. Climber Jeff Achey remarked cynically, "Better to place a ladder for a bolt than a bolt ladder." The first 15 feet are the most difficult. Work up a crack a few feet, then swing left and ascend a few feet to a downward spike. Move back right and climb to a bolt at the top of a flake-crack. Work up and left.

Cosmosis. 5.10a or b. First ascent in 1965 in winter cold by Pat Ament and Paul Mayrose. First free ascent in 1970 by Duncan Ferguson and Bob Poling. Ascend the obvious, large, right-facing dihedral near the center of the west face of Bell Buttress.

Verve. 5.13. First led (after top-roping) by Christian Griffith, in 1986. The route, attempted first by Dale Goddard and Mark Sonnenfeld, is one of the most futuristic lines in the Boulder area. Christian describes the route as "two boulder problems separated by 30 feet of 5.12a climbing." This awesome sport-climb, with bolts, is located on the outer corner (protruding arete) just left (northwest) of the Cosmosis dihedral. Apparently many attempts were made to top-rope this route by Christian in his attempts to master the moves sufficiently to later lead them.

North Face. 5.9+ or 5.10a. First led in the late '60s by Larry Dalke. The line will be found, up the dark north side, following a steep ramp to a belay stance, then going up an aesthetic, thin crack.

The High Energy Crag

Nine miles up Boulder Canyon, as the road turns briefly to the south, and on the left (east) side of the road, is this small crag situated near the river and having a demanding overhang across its full length. Many excellent, short routes exist.

Star Span. 5.11 b or c. Climbed on-sight with a top-rope in 1976 by Pat Ament, then led a few days later by Ament. Bob Godfrey writes in *CLIMB!*, "Mistakenly identified in climbing literature as a has-been, Ament, as unpredictable as ever, surprised the climbing community in 1976 by getting back in top shape. He... put up a new short climb, Star Span (an overhanging crack reminiscent of Supremacy), of considerable technical difficulty, which effectively repulsed a number of the young hot shots of the seventies" (it didn't surprise anyone when Ament was out of shape again, a week later). The true surprise is the finish of this overhanging hand-crack, where the crack turns less-than-vertical and looks as though it should be easy but isn't.

Coney Island Cliff

This obscure, double-level rock is found high above the road, on the right (north) side, about nine miles up Boulder Canyon. The rock is a kind of western appendage of Easter Rock. There exist many sport-climbs now on this rock, some on the lower tier and some on the upper wall. Reeperbahn, one of the most difficult sport-climbs on this rock (5.13b), ascends the upper wall, to the left of Quintet, via eight bolts.

Quintet. 5.10. First ascent in 1978 by Scott Woodruff and Dan Hare. Near the left side of the upper level of the rock is a prominent, right-facing dihedral (a route called Loading Zone). To the right of this dihedral, find a smaller dihedral (with six roofs). Start on a flake to the right. Step left at the largest roof. The 2nd pitch follows the dihedral.

Coney Island Baby. 5.11d or 5.12a. First ascent in 1982 by Erik Erickson and Mark Rolofson. Mark recalls, "Both climbers took 15-foot falls, attempting the pitch, on a tricky-to-place, hidden R.P. nut." This pitch climbs a right-leaning arch right of Quintet for 60 feet to a belay. Easier climbing finishes.

Castle Rock

The name was changed from "Dome Rock" (used as far back as the early 1900's) to Castle Rock. At about 11.5 miles is Boulder Canyon's best tower of granite, encircled on the south by a dirt road (the original road up the canyon).

A cruise up the road, past
"Dome Rock," before climbers --

Radio Andromeda. 5.11. First ascent in 1972 by Pat Ament and Roger Briggs. A few "tries" were required on the first ascent to clean bushes, dirt, and lichen. The climb became one of Castle Rock's best, as lichen was replaced by flesh, and ascends the steep (partly overhanging) east wall of Castle Rock. The first pitch (**the First Movement**) was done on aid in 1962 by Stan Shepard and Greg Blomberg and was done free in 1972 by Jim Erickson and Pat Ament. It is the shallow groove/crack running vertically up the wall, starting a short distance northwest of the bridge. In high water, it is difficult to get to the start of this pitch. The easy-looking groove is 5.10. Originally led free with wildly-spaced, scary, hex nuts, it now is protected well with smaller "friends." About 50 feet up, look for an obscure traverse around a corner to the south, across a steep, thin slab (5.11-), and arrive at a small stance below the crux, overhanging crack. For help, one must radio Andromeda.

Tourist Extravagance. 5.12d or 5.13a? First ascent in 1962 by Bob Boucher and Bob Sandafer. Led free all but the crux start in 1981 by Jeff Achey. Led all free in 1985 by Christian Griffith. This was perhaps the first 5.13 route in the Boulder area. Christian used two different types of shoes. West of the bridge, at the southeast corner of Castle Rock, a wall begins as a vertical slab with a bolt. Climb this (the crux) to a flake-ledge. Above, climb vertically up the small crack and a roof. Find an amazing traverse left, around a corner to the small belay shelf called "the bar" on Country Club Crack.

Country Club Crack. 5.11c. First ascent in 1956 by Ted Rouillard and Cleve McCarty. Led free in 1967 by Pat Ament (with Mike Stults and Tom Ruwitch). Only two bolts were used on the original aid ascent, one on the 1st pitch and one just over the roof near the top. On the smooth, initial wall, a shoulder-stand was employed. During an age of disputed ethics and incompetent climbers, bolts were added to the first wall. These bolts were chopped and then replaced, then chopped and replaced again, an ugly testimony of ego connected to one of the most beautiful free-climbs in the country.

Ted Rouillard on the first ascent
of Country Club Crack in 1956
photo by Cleve McCarty

Historically, Chuck Pratt in about 1963 or early '64 was the first to free-climb the initial moves, from the fingertip undercling reaching upward and right but not having protection or finding the necessary hold. The free ascent was in the grasp of Royal Robbins in 1964 who, without chalk, made it all free in twilight except for two points at the top of the route. He top-roped the initial wall after first demonstrating that it could be aided without the use of any bolts (A4). On the free ascent in 1967, Tom Ruwitch replaced one of the old bolts (which was about to fall out), moving it a few feet left to a location more strategic in terms of the free line. In 1967, the initial wall was perhaps only 5.11a. A hold broke a bit, leaving the hold smaller and slightly more difficult to use. Start directly across from the south end of the bridge, just right (northeast) of a pointed flake of rock. The route is obvious, starting with a difficult, smooth wall with two bolts and becoming a series of vertical, left-arching cracks up an impressive wall. The 1st pitch ends at a small shelf on the right of the crack, about 70 feet up. This shelf, called "the bar," ties into the name of the route which was derived from the brand of beverage consumed during the original aid ascent. Those first climbers recall a young sorority girl below on the ground who took great caution in lieu of a restroom to find a secluded spot. Scanning in all directions and sure of privacy, she settled below Country Club Crack. At this point, both climbers sang an appropriate song.... The 2nd pitch continues up the ever-steepening crack, over an exhausting-looking but actually moderate roof, and up the final crux -- a left-leaning, shallow hand-jam. This last short but sweet section above the roof was made easier by the creative Roger Briggs who discovered a knee-lock rest (in the hole just above the roof, with left knee in, facing right).

Athlete's Feat. 5.11a. First ascent in 1961 by Stan Shepard and Don Davis. First free ascent in 1964 by Royal Robbins and Pat Ament. Third pitch done free in 1964 by Dave Rearick and Pat Ament. With three 5.10 pitches, one 5.11 pitch, and a choice of 5.9 or 5.10 cracks to exit, each pitch on excellent rock, this is one of the best routes in Boulder. In 1964, the 1st pitch (the crux) was done without any bolt for protection and no chalk. Royal wore shoes called "Spiders." At the difficult move, he risked a long fall down onto a pointed spike of rock. It has been suggested that this pitch was the hardest in the country at the time, apart from John Gill's difficult boulders in the Tetons and the Needles of South Dakota. Bolts were later added to the pitch by less scrupulous climbers wishing a safer sense (i.e. the achievement but without the risk). Although one of the holds above the initial mantel later deteriorated slightly and became harder to use, the level of difficulty is not far from what it first was.

Scramble to the top of a large, pointed spike of rock that rests against the wall left of the start of Country Club and a short distance southwest of the bridge. Undercling up and left, then do the crux moves over a short, bulging wall onto an obvious, large, slanting shelf. Scramble easily to the left to a belay stance at the base of an overhanging crack. The 2nd pitch liebacks and jams up the obvious, rounded crack above. Reach a large, sloping ledge for a belay. The 3rd pitch is a short but fierce lieback-jam up the next obvious, overhanging crack. First done free in 1964 by David Rearick and Pat Ament, this is the psychological crux of the route -- certainly now that the first pitch is well protected. When Rearick led it, he fell as he moved over the top lip of the crack and went head first toward the ledge. Ament pulled in rope and caught him an inch from hitting his head on the ledge. Rearick did not wait for the experience to psyche him out and led up again, succeeding.

The 4th pitch is deceptively easy-looking. Ament recalls leading the pitch and hearing Royal, who was belaying below, ask, "Why are you moving so slow, isn't that 4th class?" The pitch is minimal 5.10, ending on a good shelf. Either move left (west) along the shelf to a 5.8+ hand-jam up an inside-corner or go straight up a left-curving, 5.9+ hand-crack in a steep wall. The 5.9+ variation was done in 1968 by Ament, Tom Ruwitch, and Roger Briggs.

Never A Dull Moment. 5.12-. First ascent in 1979 by Alec Sharp and Andy Parkin. Start a short distance left of the start of Athelte's Feat and even closer to (just right of) the start of Jackson's Wall Direct. Traverse right, across a steep wall with bolts and using a finger-nail hold. Continue right, along a difficult, sloping foothold system, and make some moves upward to reach the left end of the big, sloping ledge at the top of the 1st pitch of Athlete's Feat. Belay here. Move up and left, around the awkward corner, and ascend the vertical, difficult hand/finger/lieback/jam-crack to the ledge at the top of the 2nd pitch of Athlete's Feat. This much is the best of the route, although one may do two more pitches that were a part of the original ascent. The 3rd pitch moves left, then works up and right (past a bolt), to a small dihedral which is climbed. The 4th pitch (difficult to protect) ascends a rib left of Athlete's Feat. At one point, move left and up a ramp.

CASTLE ROCK
4. COUNTRY CLUB CRACK
5. ATHLETE'S FEAT
6. JACKSON'S WALL DIRECT
7. TONGO
8. JACKSON'S WALL
9. CUSSIN CRACK
8
9
8
7
6
4
5
CMc '65

Jackson's Wall Direct. 5.9+. First ascent in 1961 by George Hurley and Charles Roskosz. First led free in the mid-'60s by Layton Kor. Another name suggested by the first ascent party was Wilmon's Wall, after Prince Wilmon who was first to discover the line and who pushed it to the final vertical wall. This route follows the most obvious line up the south face of Castle Rock. Forty or Fifty feet up the hill southwest from the start of Country Club Crack, find an obvious crack that arches upward to the right in a right-facing dihedral. Climb about 15 or 20 feet up to the crack and lieback it a short distance to where it is possible to move left around the corner (a hidden hold is found out on the wall to the left). Get onto a small shelf and traverse the shelf left to an optional belay stance. From the west end of the stance, continue west across steep, somewhat unprotected slabs to a thin crack that leads upward to a good belay ledge. The second lead goes straight up, above the right end of the belay ledge, passing a big flake (or block). Ascend up and slightly right via a steep flake to a small, sloping stance. Move up and right, onto a tiny mantel-shelf, and make a very delicate balance traverse left (slightly upward) across a vertical wall (with small, unseen holds). Protection is difficult over this section and runout. Continue left and up to join the regular Jackson's Wall route at a shelf below its final, steep wall.

The Gill Crack. 5.12a. First ascent bouldered in the mid-'60s by John Gill. To the immediate right of some rock made black by picnic fires, find a vertical finger crack.

Tongo. 5.10d or 5.11a. First ascent in 1963 by Pat Ament and Will Bassett. First free ascent in 1967 by Pat Ament and Roger Briggs. Start just left of a large tree, not far left of a black smoke streak made by campfires. The 1st lead of the route is an obvious, right-angling, thin ramp system that acts as a rounded hold for an extended hand-traverse up and right -- to a belay shelf. This lead is the psychological crux, since it is slightly runout and strenuous to protect, while the short 2nd pitch has moves more difficult. Immediately off the ground, start with a long reach to an undercling hold. Move left a step or two, surmount the small roof in front of you, and angle up and right a few moves. Here is a bolt, although no bolts were placed or used on the first ascent or first free ascent. Move left and upward a step or two to a stance and begin the hand-traverse upward and right along the sloping "ramp." Reach a shelf that serves as a good belay. From the right end of the shelf, ascend straight up to a roof with a crack that angles upward and left through the roof. This is the crux, although well protected by nuts. From a good belay shelf a short distance above the roof, move up and right (to join Jackson's Wall Direct, or traverse left along ledges, twice dropping downward along the ledge, and find the obvious gully/trough which can be ascended or descended).

Acrobat Overhang. 5.12. First ascent in the mid-'60s by the greatest boulderer of all time, John Gill. This short problem is high enough to be considered more than a bouldering route. The dangerous landing requires control and serious consideration. Left (west) of the start of Tongo and just left of a wide crack is an obvious, bulging wall with horizontal finger-cracks running through it. Hand-traverse left, out the highest of the two horizontal cracks and make a difficult move up and left around an imposing bulge to a hold. Somehow get onto the hold.

Cussin' Crack. 5.6+. First known ascent in the early '50s by Harold Walton, et al. Walton found a piton in the climb and only could assume the route had been done previously. The derivation of the name is from some utterances articulated by a normally soft-spoken individual impinged in the crack (Harold Walton). The route begins at the southwest side of the rock at the obvious, wide opening of rock -- a kind of chimney/cave. Climb any of several ways to the very prominent, right-angling trough above. Quickly begin looking for a traverse left, along a balance ledge across a steep wall. Near the end of the ledge, a short, difficult move brings one to a big ledge. Gain another ledge slightly higher and to the west. Above this ledge is the big dihedral called Cussin' Crack: slippery and harder than it looks. The dihedral ends with a steep, inside-corner wall.

The Campaigner. 5.12. An aid route in early days, led free in 1980 by Jeff Achey. A pivotal climb of the era, of substantial difficulty, this is a right-slanting, overhanging, awkward, hand/finger-crack that curves up and out through the lower right side of the big practice roof (the huge roof) on the southwest side of Castle Rock.

Rebellion. 5.12. First ascent in 1986 led by Mark Rolofson. A subtle but beautiful achievement, this ascends a short, left-leaning seam (dihedral) just to the right (east) of Campaigner. Near the top of the crack, exit onto the sloping shelf left. "Every move is 5.11," said a climber attempting it one day.

The Coffin Crack. 5.10b. First ascent in 1964 by David Rearick and Pat Ament. This is the shallow, overhanging slot one crack left of the big Practice Roof, on the southwest side of Castle Rock. The crux is the slot, although the route was done as a continuous line all the way to the top of the rock. To climb only the bottom slot, a loop of sling (with a carabiner) can be placed around a flake after leading the slot. Then flip the sling off.

The Final Exam. 5.11a. First ascent in 1964 by Royal Robbins and Pat Ament. The name was derived when, as Robbins began up the crux, a tourist in her eighties yelled from a car, "That must be the final exam."

Royal Robbins leading the Final Exam, 1964

photo by Pat Ament

This was another of Royal's impressive leads, done on the suspicion John Gill had bouldered it (Gill had not but later bouldered it in 1964 or 1965). Located a few steps left (west) of the huge roof (overhang) on the southwest side of Castle Rock, this route involves a short, fierce, bulging wall that is pierced by a vertical crack and crossed by two horizontal cracks. The bulge is topped by a saving knob. On the first ascent, done chalkless, Royal used only one piton -- located below the crux. The route can now be protected well by nuts and often is top-roped. Most people simply down-climb cracks to the left, after finishing the route.

Curving Crack. 5.9+ or 5.10a. First ascent in 1961 by Tink Wilson, et al. First free ascent in 1964 in a snowstorm by Pat Ament and Dave Rearick. This crescent crack is seen just left of the Final Exam. The crack curves upward left and is streaked with black. The crack ends with a crux move, followed by an exit left onto a sloping shelf. Move above the shelf to another ledge. To descend from the ledge, climb left and up on easy rock, go around a corner left and down a short ramp. Scramble up to a tree and traverse left (north) to a good ledge. Drop down a gully a few steps and scramble up a ramp-crack to easy descent ledges on the north side.

Skunk Crack (also called West Slot). 5.9. First ascent in 1960 by Harvey Carter and Cary Huston. Two cracks left of Curving Crack is the obvious inside-corner that offers a slippery lieback 20 feet to a downward-flaring chimney/slot.

Comeback Crack. 5.10b or c. Free ascent in 1972 by Pat Ament and Jim Erickson. Originally full of grass and dirt, the free ascent was more difficult than the route now is. This is the vertical, hand/finger crack a couple feet right of Skunk Crack.

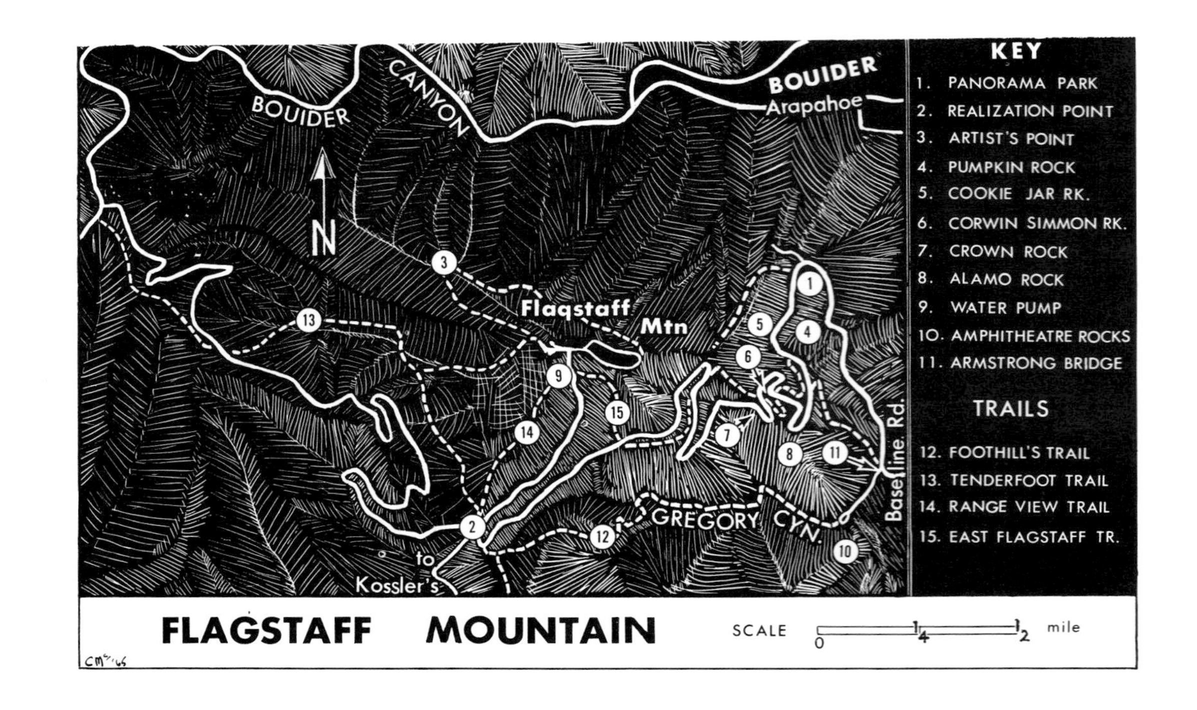
BOULDER CANYON
BOULDER
Arapahoe
N
Flagstaff Mtn
GREGORY CYN.
Base line Rd.
to Kossler's
KEY
1. PANORAMA PARK
2. REALIZATION POINT
3. ARTIST'S POINT
4. PUMPKIN ROCK
5. COOKIE JAR RK.
6. CORWIN SIMMON RK.
7. CROWN ROCK
8. ALAMO ROCK
9. WATER PUMP
10. AMPHITHEATRE ROCKS
11. ARMSTRONG BRIDGE
TRAILS
12. FOOTHILL'S TRAIL
13. TENDERFOOT TRAIL
14. RANGE VIEW TRAIL
15. EAST FLAGSTAFF TR.
FLAGSTAFF MOUNTAIN
SCALE 0 1/4 1/2 mile

FLAGSTAFF MOUNTAIN

The ever-popular boulders of Flagstaff Mountain have long been a place of easy after-work entertainment or training. The road up Flagstaff begins at the west end of Baseline Road (Baseline runs east and west through Boulder). Mileage readings are taken at the sharp turn north where Baseline becomes the Flagstaff road.

A part of the Boulder Mountain Parks, Flagstaff is constantly threatened by those who have no awareness or respect for natural beauty. Destructive partiers frequently leave beer cans or bottles. Bottles are illegal in the park. It behooves the climber to remove some of the trash. Another problem, due in part to the number of climbers, is route deterioration. Climbers must be sensitive to the rock and to the friableness of certain flakes and holds. With care, holds on the verge of breaking can survive indefinitely. It is also important not to contribute to erosion along the base of rocks, and foliage can be destroyed if there is no effort to preserve it. Rubber buildup on footholds is minimized by precise technique and by avoiding uncontrolled slip-offs.

Because boulder routes are difficult to rate, because people vary in size and reach, and because something so small as humidity may play a role in difficulty, there is no perfect rating system. The standard of difficulty, ultimately, becomes less important than one's personal standard and one's interests. Thus this section of the book excludes ratings and lets the difficulty be determined by direct experience (or else imagination). Certainly a few of the most difficult routes fall into the 5.12 to 5.13, even 5.14, range, while some of the most worthwhile and classic routes may be as easy as 5.8. Included here are a few of the more historical, well known, or classic routes. Of course the following routes are a small sample of the many good routes on Flagstaff Mountain.

"An actual ascent of a route is a unique climb, never to be re-experienced on succeeding ascents, even if the same technique is used over and over again. Each ascent is distinctive and part of a developing pattern. Wiring a route, seen through a traditionalist's eye, is a boulderer's trick. Within another paradigm, however, a design emerges, decorated with the highly colored embroidery of kinesthetic awareness, one of the mystical rewards of bouldering."
-- John Gill, June 1979

Northwest Overhang of Pumpkin Rock. This rock is located among trees at the south end of a meadow, a few hundred yards south of a small, stone shelter near the Flagstaff House Restaurant. The northwest overhang is an old practice aid-climb whose wholes are where pitons once were placed. These holes serve as slots for fingers. The route is an excellent top-rope problem that tests the forearms. Large, steel eye-bolts on top of the rock can be reached by a simple route on the south side.

West Face of Pumpkin. First ascent in 1968 by Pat Ament. This is a short, overhanging wall above a ledge, following a shallow inset of rock. Start by stepping up with the left foot to a small, quartz pebble (frictioning with left hand on the inset).

Cookie Jar Crack. A short distance west and uphill from Pumpkin, Cookie Jar is the first boulder on the right side of the road as the road heads south from the Flagstaff House Restaurant. The obvious crack on the south wall is one of the oldest routes around Boulder, a beginner's test that can be top-roped. Speculation has it that the first female ascent of Cookie Jar Crack was made in the early '50s by Betty Armstrong -- an event that made the Boulder newspaper.

The Shield. This is the bulging wall immediately to the right of Cookie Jar Crack, excellently steep but reasonable climbing.

Jackson's Pitch. First ascent apparently by Dallas Jackson. This ascends the obvious, large bulge on the north side of Cookie Jar Rock, starting with a type of undercling with the right hand and reaching up and left for a small, hidden hold.

Northcutt's Roll. Presumably Ray Northcutt made the route (later 1950's) after he fell into the road off the route. The route ascends the left (south) side of the east overhang of Cookie Jar. The road has been cut away since the first ascent, presenting serious exposure.

North Face of Corwin Simmons Rock. First ascent in the 1950's by Corwin Simmons. Located at the west edge of a curve about a mile and a half up the Flagstaff Road is this small spire. The north face, a wall tapering at its top, was done in heavy mountain boots.

Just Right. First ascent in 1973 by Jim Holloway. This very difficult route ascends the southeast overhang of Capstan Rock -- a spire located a couple hundred feet north of Corwin Simmons Rock, 1.55 miles up the road. Capstan has a distinctive horn at its top sometimes used for top-rope anchoring. At six-foot-four, Holloway found the holds spaced "just right" (out of reach of everyone else).

The Consideration. First ascent in 1969 by Pat Ament. This ascends the left side of a bulging wall near the right (east) end of

Dave Rearick bouldering on Capstan Rock,
Flagstaff, early 1960's / photo by Pat Ament

the formation called Cloud Shadow -- a south-facing wall down the road-bank east from Capstan Rock. Start right of (but avoid) a large hole (pocket) one is tempted to use with the left hand.

Hagan's Wall. First ascent in the late 1960's by Paul Hagan. Toward the west end of Cloud Shadow Rock is a difficult, bulging wall. Starting just right (east) of a tree, and climb up (slightly right) near the center of this rounded wall.

Dandy Lion. First ascent in the early 1980's by Dan Stone. Just a few inches left of Hagan's Wall is an imposing, difficult route.

A.H.R. (Another Holloway Route). First ascent in the early/mid-1970's by Jim Holloway. This very challenging route goes straight over the prominently bulging overhang just to the right (east) of the Consideration. The only known second ascent of the route, via a slightly easier variation, was done in the early 1990's by Ben Moon.

Jim Holloway begins his route Just Right -- photo by Pat Ament

Bob Horan, Hagan's Wall / photo by Jim Sanders

Jim Holloway begins his route "A.H.R." on Flagstaff / photo by Pat Ament

Hollow's Way. First ascent in 1975-1976 by Bob Candelaria. This difficult route goes up the center of the north wall of Notlim Boulder. This boulder is found by walking north, downhill, several hundred feet from Capstan Rock.

The Right-Hand Mantel. First ascent in 1966 by Pat Ament. Just east of the parking area near Crown Rock, 1.66 miles up the road, are two boulders that sit together -- called the One-Arm Rocks. A number of routes were done by Pat Ament, Richard Smith, and Bob Kamps where only one arm was allowed. The best ascends the north face of the westerly rock, a difficult, one-arm reach, then mantel onto a small shelf, followed by a balance move (still one arm) to get standing on the shelf).

Ament does the Right-Hand Mantel
photo by Christian Griffith --

Pratt's Mantel and Pratt's Overhang. From the Crown Rock parking area 1.66 miles up the Flagstaff road, walk along a path south a few hundred feet to a rock facing west with overhangs. Pratt's Mantel (the shelf on the left/north side) and Pratt's Overhang (the right-slanting groove up through the overhang) were named after -- although not climbed by -- the inimitable Yosemite master Chuck Pratt. The first known ascent of Pratt's Overhang occurred in about 1960 by Bob Culp.

Smith Overhang. First ascent in 1967 by 6-foot-5 Richard Smith. This is the overhanging wall a few inches to the right (south) of Pratt's Overhang. The ground has eroded some, and the first flake for the left hand has broken and been glued back more than once.

Crystal Corner. First known ascent in the early '60s by Bob Culp. This is the overhanging arete/corner a few inches to the right of Smith Overhang.

The Gill Swing. First ascent in the late '60s by John Gill. This starts with the right hand pinching a rounded hold near the start of Crystal Corner and then is an aerial move from the ground to the top!

John Gill in Boulder in the 1960's / photo by Pat Ament

The Long Traverse (Monkey Traverse). This faces west, a few paces south of (downhill from) Pratt's Overhang area.
The Williams Mantel. First ascent in 1969 by Bob Williams. From the Long Traverse, amble downhill south past a square-ish boulder sitting by itself and find the sloping west end of the next rock south.
The Ament Eliminate. First ascent in 1964 by Pat Ament. Around the corner southeast from the Williams Mantel is a short, west-facing bulge with a vertical crack at its left and a horizontal crack angling slightly upward left. From the handhold at the top of the overhang, right of the vertical crack, go straight up not using the vertical crack or another undercling-finger-crack that angles up right.
Southwest Corner of Beer Barrel Rock. Beer Barrel is a short walk downhill south (slightly west) from the Crown Rock parking area and below (west, slightly north, of) Pratt's Overhang. It is west of a picnic table. The southwest corner is a delightful overhang.

Bob Poling on the Poling Pebble Route on Beer Barrel / photo by Pat Ament

Poling Pebble Route. First ascent in 1968 by Bob Poling. This climbs the right side of the south wall of Beer Barrel, ending on the

east slabs at least a foot or so right of the obvious summit block. The critical pebble, located on the steepest part of the bulging wall, and used for the left hand, has broken off but been put back on with epoxy and may or may not be there still.

Tree Slab. Below and southwest of Beer Barrel is a west-facing slab. The obvious route up the center is a classic with many variations, including one by Pat Ament in 1970 using one hand.

Navajo Crack. This route is one of the few off-width type crack climbs on Flagstaff, located on the west face of Alamo at Alamo's lower south end. Alamo Rock is reached by walking south several hundred yards from the Crown Rock parking area (1.66 miles up the road), skirting left (east) around the Pratt's Overhang rocks and persisting until Alamo is seen as the largest flatiron-type formation.

The Tear-Drop Route. First ascent in the mid-1960's by Pat Ament. This ascends the overhanging wall a few inches left (north) of Navajo Crack. Part way up the wall is a hole or depression that resembles the shape of a tear-drop.

Legacy Of The Kid. First ascent in 1974 by Bob Candelaria (and dedicated to one of the best boulderers, David Breashears). The Candel Area, named after Candelaria who in the mid-1970's did many routes here, is located a short distance southeast and downhill from Alamo Rock. The area itself is slightly removed from the populated main areas and offers several formations of good rock. The route, Legacy Of The Kid, is located on a small spire's steep northwest wall, just right of an obvious, southwest-facing ramp (also a good route). Legacy begins by climbing an obvious red streak (a separate route in itself) and then finishes high on the northwest wall above the red streak.

Bob Candelaria
Photo by
Pat Ament

The Classic Undercling on the Pebble Wall. The first rock uphill north of the Crown Rock parking area is the Pebble Wall. The moderate but steep classic ascends the right side of the south wall, starting at the northwest end of a smaller boulder sitting at the southeast end of Pebble Wall. The route ends with hands jammed palm-up under a down-hanging flake.

Crystal Mantel. First done with the right arm, facing left, by Pat Ament in the mid-1960's. Near the center of the south face of Pebble Wall is an obvious quartz crystal protruding from the rock, about head-high when standing at the bottom. The crystal can be surmounted facing right (east), using the left arm, the easier way, or facing left -- much more difficult. In the mid-1970's, Jim Holloway did the mantel straight on, facing the rock, using both hands. Once standing on the crystal, the remainder of the route to the top (straight up and slightly left) is a bit high off the ground.

Direct South Face. First done in the mid-1960's by Pat Ament. This starts a step or two west of the Crystal Mantel, with hands on two good, large crystals and the right foot high up in a shallow scoop.

Guerin Traverse. First ascent in the later-1970's by Skip Guerin. This is a very challenging, low-level traverse across the entire length of the Pebble Wall's south side. Rumor has it that Layton Kor in the 1960's did some kind of traverse of the Pebble Wall.

Standard Route on the Red Wall. First known ascent in the early '60s by Bob Culp. A short distance uphill northeast from Pebble Wall, past one boulder (The North Rock) is a south-facing, vertical wall with finger pockets and pebbles. The classic route begins with the left foot near a worn tree root. Go straight up the middle.

Right Side of the Red Wall. First ascent in 1967 by Pat Ament. This is the best route on the wall. A few inches left of the tree, look for a pocket high up on the wall near the top. This is the goal. The route starts with fingertips of the left hand in a shallow pocket overhead (Bob Williams tried gluing his fingers to this with Duco cement). Two fingertips of the right hand sit in a tiny hole lower. The right foot sets precariously in a slippery hole that becomes more or sometimes less difficult to stand on as one pulls up. Between the starting holds and the higher pocket is another small crystal reached with the fingertips of the right hand.

Varney Direct. First ascent in the late '60s by Eric Varney. Between the Standard Route and the Right Side (of the Red Wall), start with the right hand in the hole used by the left hand when starting the Right Side. The left hand pinches a small crystal....

Pat Ament climbing the
Right Side of the Red Wall,
on Flagstaff

The Overhanging Hand-Traverse. First ascent in 1967 by Pat Ament. This route is located in the Flagstaff Amphitheater -- not the man-made amphitheater at the east summit of Flagstaff, nor the Amphitheater Rocks of Green Mountain, rather a small, natural amphitheater of sandstone opening to the south and located uphill to the north from the Pebble Wall. The inside, west-facing wall of the Flagstaff Amphitheater has an overhanging hand-traverse, starting off a sloping stone and angling upward right, to slabs above. **South Face of the Flagstaff Amphitheater**. First ascent in 1967 by Pat Ament. Locate the overhanging crack/dihedral up in the right-hand corner of the Flagstaff Amphitheater. Start fifteen feet left of this, off the left side of a sloping slab, and follow a line just to the right of a shallow, left-facing inside-corner. The first holds are two small finger-tip knobs above and to the right of the shallow inside-corner. The next hold is a pointed knob. The route, done without top-roping, offers a significant psychological challenge -- with the slab of rock and sloping ground below.

Christian Griffith bouldering on Flagstaff -- photo by Dan Corrigan

King Conquer. First ascent in the early 1960's by Pat Ament. A test-piece for its day, this overhanging hand-crack pierces the west-facing wall of a spire of rock located at the top north end of the Great Ridge. Extending uphill in a north-south direction, the Great Ridge is a long, west-facing series of walls, overhangs, spires, and cracks. The lowest end of the Great Ridge can be located by ambling northwest up a little valley to the left of the Pebble Wall. King Conquer sits at the top of this valley.

First Overhang. First ascent in 1968 by Pat Ament. This overhang is located on the south side of a boulder found just north of the second sharp switchback in the road above the Crown Rock parking area. The boulder is uphill west of the Great Ridge.

Ament -- No-friction loafers and combed hair
on First Overhang, 1967 / photo by Betsy Swan

the Third Flatiron, photo by Cleve McCarty

THE FLATIRON ROCKS

-- including Green Mountain, Skunk Canyon, Dinosaur Mountain, Bear Canyon, Fern Canyon, and Bear Mountain.

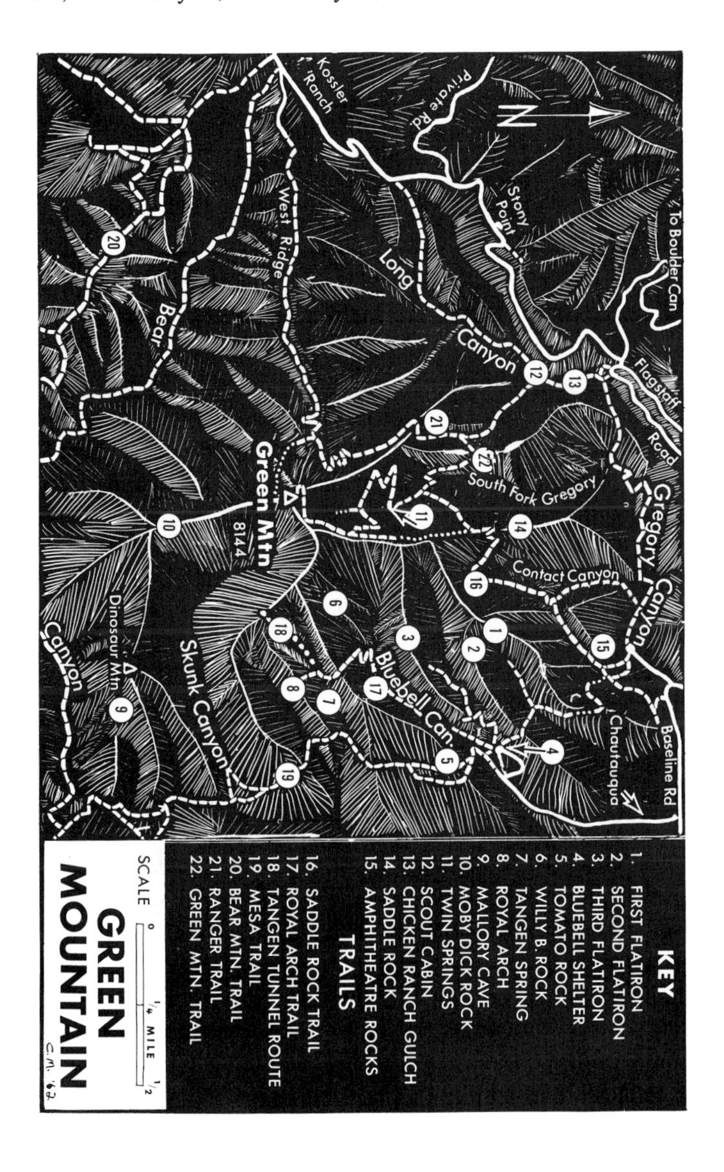

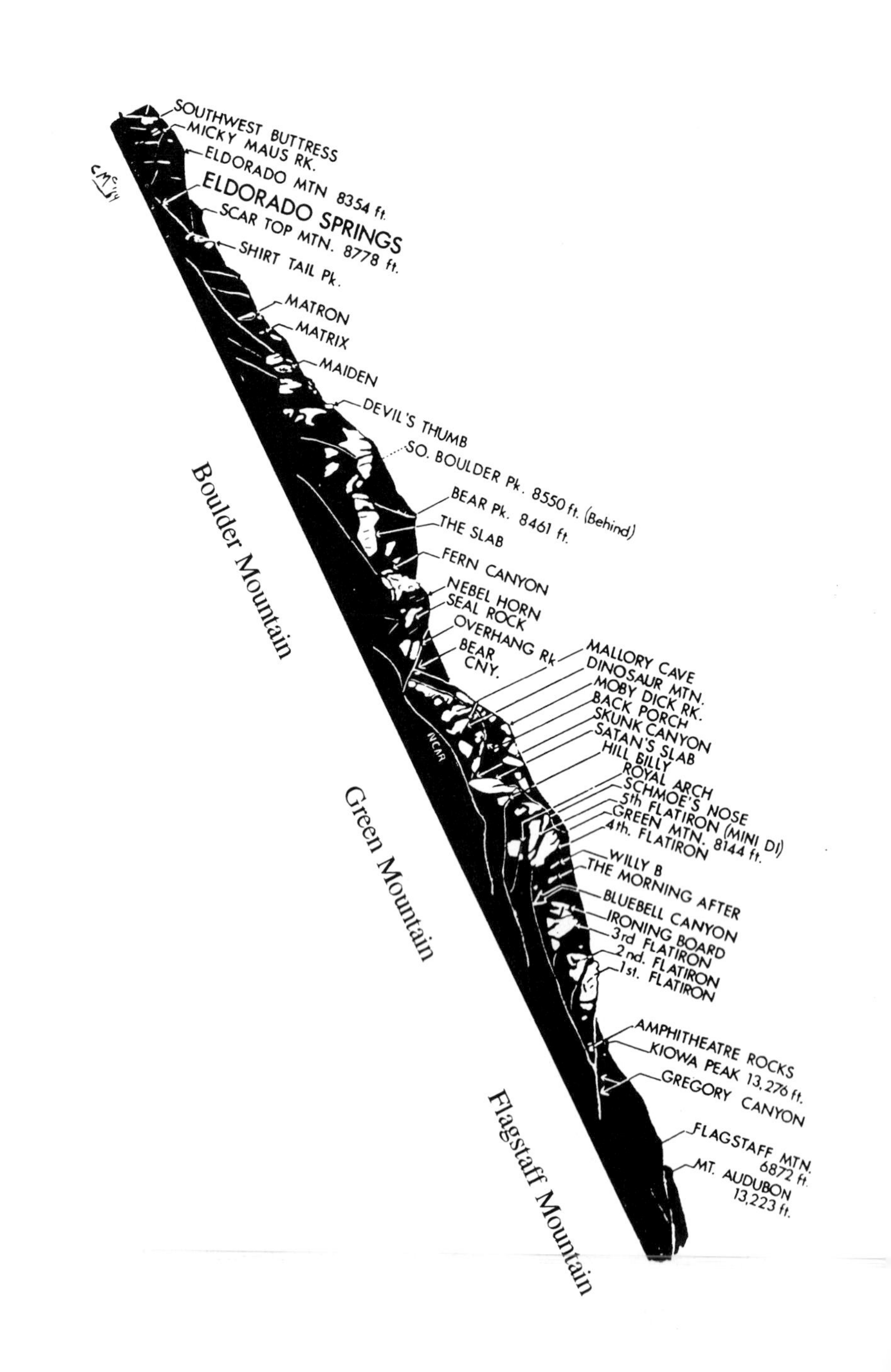
SOUTHWEST BUTTRESS
MICKY MAUS RK.
ELDORADO MTN 8354 ft.
ELDORADO SPRINGS
SCAR TOP MTN. 8778 ft.
SHIRT TAIL Pk.
MATRON
MATRIX
MAIDEN
DEVIL'S THUMB
SO. BOULDER Pk. 8550 ft. (Behind)
BEAR Pk. 8461 ft.
THE SLAB
FERN CANYON
NEBEL HORN
SEAL ROCK
OVERHANG Rk
BEAR CNY.
MALLORY CAVE
DINOSAUR MTN.
MOBY DICK RK.
BACK PORCH
SKUNK CANYON
SATAN'S SLAB
HILL BILLY
ROYAL ARCH
SCHMOE'S NOSE
5th FLATIRON (MINI DI)
GREEN MTN. 8144 ft.
4th. FLATIRON
WILLY B
THE MORNING AFTER
BLUEBELL CANYON
IRONING BOARD
3rd FLATIRON
2nd. FLATIRON
1st. FLATIRON
AMPHITHEATRE ROCKS
KIOWA PEAK 13,276 ft.
GREGORY CANYON
FLAGSTAFF MTN. 6872 ft.
MT. AUDUBON 13,223 ft.
NCAR
Boulder Mountain
Green Mountain
Flagstaff Mountain

GREEN MOUNTAIN

Seen above Chautauqua, this is the mountain with the obvious largest flatiron rocks (numbered north to south).

The Amphitheater.

The delightful pinnacles known as the Amphitheater rise out of the trees above and to the south of Gregory Canyon. A short trail from the Gregory Canyon parking circle leads into the Amphitheater -- which opens to the south.

First Pinnacle of the Amphitheater, via McCrumm's Crack. 5.5 to 5.6(?). One of the finest routes in the Amphitheater climbs the inside, right-hand wall (the west-facing wall) via obvious ledges or a corner-dihedral to a notch below a "bench." A few feet left (west) of the bench is a steep, 35 or 40-foot wall with a crack that leads to the summit of the First Pinnacle. This airy route enjoys exposure down into the Amphitheater as well as outward toward Boulder to the east. One may also finish directly above the bench.

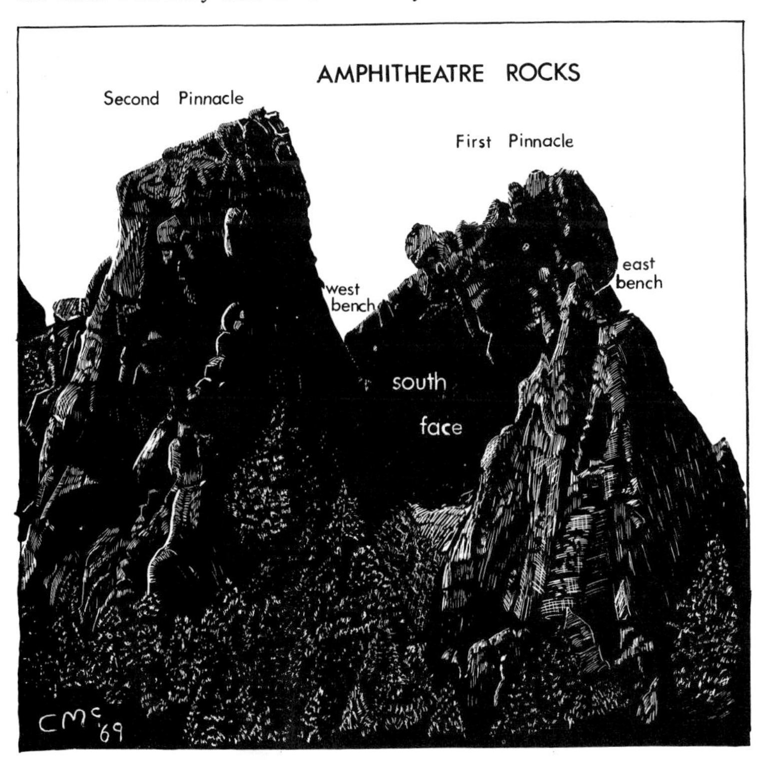

First Flatiron.

East Face. 5.4 to 5.6(?). This challenging friction ascent up the east face of the First Flatiron starts at the lowest point of the face. The most taxing friction begins at once. After two hundred or so feet, the route is more obvious and arrives at the North Arete -- itself a splendid route enjoyable for its airy suspension over Boulder and its exposure to the peaks of the Front Range.

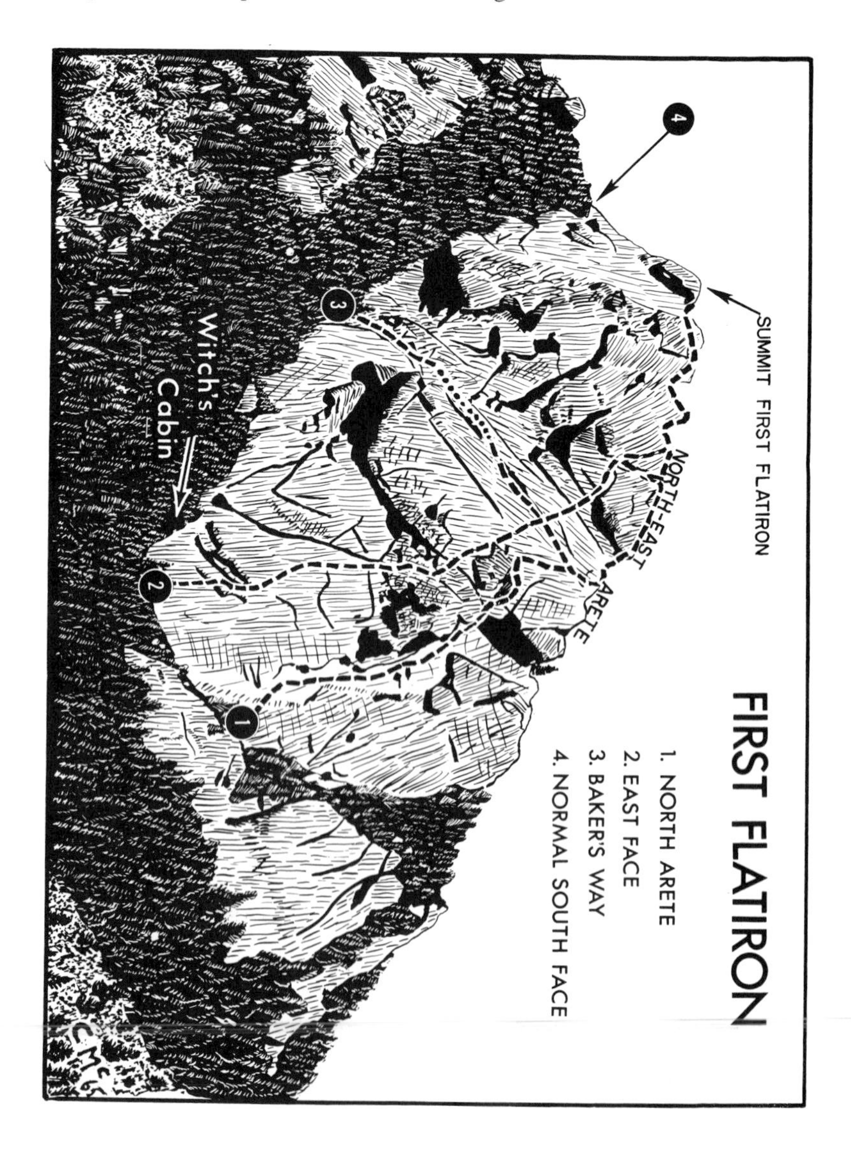

Baker's Way. 5.4 to 5.5? A route that has survived the test of time, this tours the east face of the First Flatiron to the North Arete. Only the first 40 feet are in the 5.4-5.5 rating, the remainder considerably easier. Scramble up to the Witch's Cabin, an immense boulder system that avalanched from the upper reaches perhaps centuries ago. Hike up the gully along the south edge of the east face. Two hundred feet above the Witch's Cabin, on a rock shoulder of the east face 40 feet above the ground, are two pines. The rock shoulder is the crux. Climb to the trees, then northwest on slabs. A break in a large band of rock (150 feet from the trees) allows passage over and onto the east face proper. Follow ledges diagonally up and across the face to the North Arete.

Second Flatiron.

The next rock south of the First Flatiron.

Hornsby's Ledges. 5.8+? First ascent in 1948 by David Hornsby and Harold Walton. A difficult, short free-climb for its day, this route climbs the north overhang of the Second Flatiron (see page 4). Approximately one-third the way up the right (north) side of the Pullman Car (the upper, highest block of the Second Flatiron), is an obvious fault in the rock. Two tongues of rock, one on top of the other, designate the route. Begin with a swing and work up an overhanging series of cracks to the east face. Mis-identified in early guidebooks as an aid-climb, and claimed in 1973 by Jim Erickson as a free route, the orginal party ascended the route without aid. In Harold Walton's words, "This was hard work, muscling up on those overhangs. More than once one or the other of us fell and swung out. We pounded a piton up in the corner there...."

The Third Flatiron.

Due to nesting raptors, occasional restrictions on climbing are posted for this most famous rock in the area. The rock is the most distinct, largest pinnacle of the flatirons.

East Face. 4th class-to easy 5th. First recorded ascent in 1906 by Earl and Floyd Millard. Evidence of mass enthusiasm for this rock dates back to a news clipping in the Boulder Camera, April 25,1934:

"Thirty-four people on three routes, hundreds of feet of rope, and four guides, all in a steeply inclined pocket on the Third Flatiron, made one of the most unique traffic jams known in Boulder history. Twenty-nine Revel Rangers from Denver, guided by Hull Cook and Howard Moore, were descending on the south ledges of the Third Flatiron when they encountered a small party, led by Charles Hardin, from the east chimney. Hardly had this party gotten its ropes thoroughly tangled when a third party, led by Ronald Ives, ascended the west chimney to the same point. With the ropes of the three parties intertwined like the streamers of a maypole, the three parties spent over 30 minutes getting untangled. Finally the guides took their respective parties on their way, two parties descending and the third party ascending to the summit."

In 1931, Ev and Carleton Long installed a series of eye-bolts up the middle of the east face, each about 125 feet apart (except the first two which are closer together). The bolts were employed to secure professionally guided ascents and exist as far as the left bottom of the large chimney/crack splitting the face) comprise the main line of ascent -- followed by the huge chimney, or the face to the right or left. The final ridge, exhilarating in strong wind, ascends the left (south) side of the east face.

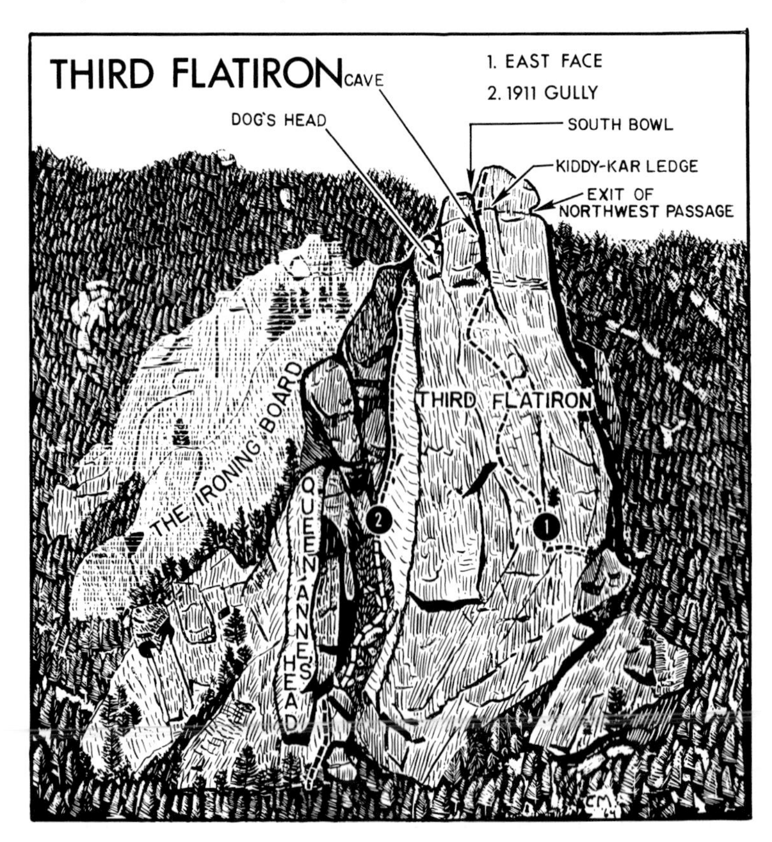

Fail Safe. 5.10+. First ascent in 1967 by Pat Ament and Gordy Ryan. This short, strenuously overhanging crack is on the west side of the Third, about 200 yards north up the obvious gully from the Royal Arch Trail. The route involves a severe arm-hand slot.

Dog's Head Cut-Off. 5.4-5.6. First ascent in 1934 by Ronald Ives. This is not a base-to-summit route up the Third Flatiron, rather a variation from the spacious trough below Slipslide Ledge (above the Southwest Chimney, on the upper southwest side of the Third). The description by Ives in a supplement to the Trail And Timberline of May, 1934, is an example of exactness and detail:

"At the northeast corner of trough above 1911 Gully and the Southwest Chimney, ascend sloping ledges until directly under large chockstones in chimney leading down from Dog's Head Rock to trough. Using right side of chockstone as right handhold and small ledge as foothold, work left across top of chockstone to right side on top. Work feet up to a small ledge on extreme left and transfer right hand to top of rock. Worm way onto chockstone until firm hold is secured, then pull body onto chockstone, and stand upright in narrow chimney, facing north. This is very awkward to do. Climb chimney, using small pockets in rock and use back and knee to toggle the narrow place. Here, raise right arm overhead, grasping small projection at extreme limit of reach, and pull body up about a foot. Pull body to sloping ledge just below Dog's Head, 55 feet above trough. From here, it is an easy climb to the Dog's Head. Angle 145 feet north across the east face and join the regular routes where they meet Kiddy Kar Ledge. Postscript: This route is impossible for anyone who cannot squeeze through a 7-inch crack."

Friday's Folly. 5.7. First ascent in 1950 by Tom Hornbein and Harry Waldrop. For many years this was the most popular, difficult climb in the Boulder region. It still retains most of its original fascination. The charm lies in the sensational elements of 90 feet and 90 degrees on near-perfect rock. Added to the steepness is an exaggerated sense of exposure where the rock and terrain fall away steeply below to the south. The route ascends the south-facing wall of the upper west buttress of the Third, beginning for about 15 feet on the actual west buttress and moving around an airy corner to a crack that is followed up the south-facing wall.

Saturday's Folly. 5.9+? First ascent in 1958 by Gerry Roach, Stan Shepard, and Jeff Wheeler. Free-climbed in 1967 by Pat Ament and Gordy Ryan. This is a direct climb of the vertical wall of the west buttress of the Third. Fifty or so feet up is a vertical, piton crack up a headwall. Start a few feet left of Friday's Folly. At the headwall with the piton crack, keep within a left hand's reach of the crack. The route ends at the Friday's Folly ledge with eye-bolts.

Northwest Passage. 5.9+. First ascent in 1949 by Tom Hornbein, Dick Sherman, and Bob Riley. Led free in 1972 by Roger Briggs. Boulder was introduced for the first time to an overhanging aid-climb on a then seemingly impossible face (see page 5 of this book). The route starts at the lower left (north) side of the west buttress of the Third Flatiron and crosses the imposing north wall, ending in the obvious notch at the east face. Originally, soft-steel wafers and army angles afforded dubious security on the climbing and at belays. Pendulum technique was used for the second men (Sherman and Hornbein) to cross the steep slab of "Skid Row." The first ascent team lassoed a point of rock, and Riley prusiked to the final overhang where pitons were hammered and a foot-loop was employed as an aid-sling.

Bob Riley grapples with the overhang on Northwest Passage, 1949 -- photo by Tom Hornbein

Ironing Boards

These are the flat slabs west of (behind) the Third Flatiron. Many and perhaps countless routes exist. The east face of the largest Ironing Board has a route that wanders up it, often on friction climbing and runout but never terribly difficult. The pinnacle near the top of these rocks (and above the Third Flatiron to the west) is called Green Thumb.

Green Corner. 5.9. First ascent in 1969 by Roger Briggs and Don Peterson. Obvious crack on the northwest corner of Green Thumb.

The Raven. 5.11. First ascent led in 1981 by Skip Guerin. Downhill to the south from Green Corner, find an obvious (vertical), left-facing corner. Start below this and climb it.

Slave To The Rhythm. 5.13b? First ascent led in 1987 by Dan Michael. Roughly 100 yards south, down the talus gully, from the west side of Green Thumb is this sport-climb with 8 bolts.

Honemaster Lombada. 5.13d. First ascent led in 1991 by Colin Lantz. A bit right of Slave To The Rhythm, this route overhangs for 30 of its 75 feet. Knee-locks are involved on the boulder-problem start. This is followed by a 5.13a pebble traverse. The final 50 feet involve thin face climbing, ending with a lunge.

Green Crack. Grade unknown. First ascent in 1958 by Gerry Roach and Stan Shepard. This chimney-crack ascends the back (west) side of the highest Ironing Board.

The Morning After (Thing, Needle's Eye)

The east face of the first pinnacle southwest (uphill) from the Ironing Boards has a distinguishing outset from whence comes the name Needle's Eye. The term Morning After originated in the 1940's. Follow the Royal Arch Trail until it starts its switchback climb to the south. Bushwack west (uphill). Descent from the summit is made by rappelling 110 feet off the west face or by down-climbing the southwest ridge.

East Face. 5.6? First ascent in 1956 by Gerry Roach and Jeff Wheeler. Begin by climbing a slab straight up to a tree. The 2nd lead is the most difficult and works around the obvious overhang, moving right, on thin friction. A belay point can be found above, near trees. The 3rd lead works straight up the face and climbs along the left (south) side of the needle's eye to a belay point. From here, continue to a large ledge and follow easy slabs to the summit.

Variation of Overhang. 5.6? First ascent in the late 1950's or 1960 by Pat Ament and Larry Dalke. Climb the overhang behind the tree.

Longest Yard. 5.10+. First ascent in 1978 by Dan Stone and Chip Chase. This is a steep route on the north face of the Morning After. Start behind a big pine. The 1st pitch is a 20-foot finger-crack with scary protection. Lieback to a belay in a groove. The 2nd pitch finishes on the overhanging bulge above.

The Willy B

A slender spire rises alone in the forest above the Morning After. Approach by hiking up along the south side of the Morning After.

East Face. 5.6-5.7? First ascent in 1948 by Tom Hornbein and Bill Braddock. Ascend the east face of the Willy B, starting at a ledge part way up. Climb 10 feet up a short, south wall to the narrow east face. Work up, using small holds, to a belay stance. The final lead goes straight up an obvious crack.

East Face, South Side. 5.8? First ascent unknown. Ament and Dalke climbed this in about 1960 and found an old piton.... This goes up the prominent, overhanging inside corner on the south side of the east face.

Spaceship

A little spire above the Willy B is seen near the top of Green Mountain (and above the top of the Fourth Flatiron.

East Face. 5.5. Climbed first in 1969 by Gerry and Barb Roach.

Fourth Flatiron.

Less distinct than the first three flatirons, this disconnected series of smooth slabs rise toward a spire, the north face of which has a remarkable climb.

Death And Transfiguration. 5.11b or c? First ascent in 1972 by Roger Briggs and Luke Studer. This impressive route ascends the sheer north wall of Green Mountain Pinnacle -- the upper part of the Fourth Flatiron (near the top of Green). A severe crack slants upward right, over a roof. Then an overhanging dihedral is climbed by lieback and stem moves to the east slabs.

Transgression. 5.12. First ascent in 1986 by Neil Cannon, Mark Sonnenfeld, and Eric Winkelman. This is the arching roof above and right of the overhang on Death And Transfiguration and serves as a very wild direct finish to that route.

Fifth Flatiron (Mini Di)

Shaped like a diamond, with a pointed summit, the Fifth Flatiron sets a striking geometric pattern. Follow the Royal Arch Trail (starting south of the Bluebell shelter). The rock is located above (west of) the Royal Arch. Cut uphill and west off the trail, before reaching the arch.

Standard East Face. 5.5. This is a very nice climb, worth adding as a finish to the pleasant scenery of the Royal Arch Trail. Start on the right (north) side of the east face, to the left (south) of a long chimney/crack. Climb upward to the right, over a thin bulge, to a belay stance. Work diagonally upward left to a good belay point. The route then leads diagonally right, to a belay stance near the crest of the north ridge. Finish by following the ridge to the summit.

To descend, rappel 75 feet off the west side.

Schmoe's Nose.

High along the top ridge of Green Mountain, south of the summit and above the Fifth Flatiron, find this block -- shaped more like a hippo than a schmoe. What IS a schmoe?

North Face. Grade unknown. First ascent in 1951 by Cliff Chittim, Jim and John Vickery, and Karl Gustafson. Karl relates how the climb was achieved: "Throw rope over the lower of two knobs on the north face. The knob has a flat top, and one must be careful to secure the rope. On the first ascent, a smaller rope was thrown over the knob first, pulling then the climbing rope over. Climb hand-over-hand up the rope. Reach right and do a short hand-traverse to a large ledge leading to the back of the rock. Climb easily from there to the summit."

Skunk Canyon.

To reach this area, walk the Mesa Trail south, well past the old quarry (seen above the trail), or approach from NCAR (National Center for Atmospheric Research). See maps on pages 71 and 72.

The Guardian. 5.13a. Top-roped in 1987 by Bob Horan. Bob later aided up with hooks and "friends" to place bolts. He returned and led to the lip but fell. Dan McQuade led it (after earlier top-ropings). Horan "flashed" it the next day. This is in Skunk Canyon, on the first rock on the right (the obvious, overhanging wall), and is a "sporty" display of the styles of an era.

Satan's Slab. 5.8+. First ascent in 1963 by Layton Kor and Pat Ament. This was the first route in Skunk Canyon and is the long, obvious arete-ridge that sweeps upward to the north out of the floor of the canyon. Scramble to the first overhang and climb a squeeze-chimney-slot through its left side. The crux is soon encountered above the slot and is a short wall somewhat difficult to protect. Above the wall, thin friction leads to a belay on a gentle slab. More and more climbing finishes at the top. Descend from the summit via a large gully on the east side.

Sidereal. 5.9. First ascent in 1975 by Scott Woodruff, Brad Gilbert, Dan Hare, and Tim Beaman. This route starts about 100 feet below the top of the talus gully that runs upward to the north in front of (east of) Satan's Slab. A smooth wall is seen above a large, undercut roof. Stand on a precarious pile of loose blocks to reach the lip. A piton of doubtful worth was fixed to protect this first section. Traverse 20 feet up right from the lip to reach a stance below a prominent, 15-foot, right-facing dihedral. Belay here. From the top of this dihedral, climb straight up steep slabs to the top.

Seventh Inning Stretch. 5.11. First ascent in 1981 by Rick Accomazzo and Christian Griffith. Start about 45 feet right of Sidereal, below the obvious roof. Climb a large overhang on large flakes past a fixed wire-nut.

Doric Dihedral. 5.12. First ascent in 1971 by Roger Briggs and Steve Nelson. Led free in 1983 by Chip Ruckgaber. Among the many exquisite, short climbs in the Skunk Canyon area, this "unfinished" route represents a standard of difficulty expressed by the best of climbers of the early 1980's. The large, right-slanting ridge of sandstone that rises upward on the north side of Skunk

Canyon is Satan's Slab. Doric Dihedral, a prominent right-facing dihedral, is found about 150 yards up along the base of the southwest face of Satan's Slab. The crux of this continuously awkward route is, apparently, a mantel at the top of the dihedral (with scary protection)!

Beware The Future. 5.13d? First ascent led in 1988 by Bob Horan, after many attempts. Top-roped by Patrick Edlinger in 1988 after a key hold broke (he rated it possibly 5.13d if not harder). Dale Goddard repeated the route and downrated it to 5.13c, suggesting the new name: **Face The Present**. This is the arete that is the left (north) side of Doric Dihedral.

The Inferno. 5.11+ or 5.12a. First ascent in 1971 by Roger and Bill Briggs. Free ascent of the first part of the route (5.10) in 1977 by Scott Woodruff and Chris Reveley. Free ascent of the entire route in 1981 by Jeff Achey and Roger Briggs. Skunk Canyon has no better line than this up the southwest face of Satan's Slab (the largest flatiron-like slab rising out of Skunk on the north side of the canyon). Past Doric Dihedral, find the next clear line. The route starts under a large overhang. Pitch one angles up and right, around the overhang (5.8), to a stance. Surmount the bulge at the base of a crack (5.10+) and continue up 30 feet to a bolt. Pass another bulge (5.10), then move up and right. Belay carefully in an eagle's nest. Pitch two climbs up and right, around the very unlikely-looking overhang. Two bolts protect the crux (5.11+? or harder). Belay on a small stance above the overhang. The 3rd pitch follows a thin crack (shallow corner, 5.10, with tricky protection in places) to the summit. As mentioned, this route has an eagle's nest. One should not attempt the route during nesting season (June through August), although restrictions are sometimes posted by park rangers.

Third Eye. 5.9+. First ascent in 1971 by Roger Briggs and Steve Nelson. Free ascent in 1973 by Roger Briggs and Mark Hesse. One of the fun routes in Skunk Canyon, this ascends the wall across Skunk Canyon to the south of Satan's Slab. The wall goes by the name of... **Achean Pronouncement**. Find a prominent chimney and obtuse dihedral system that pierces the entire northwest face. Climb to the right of the chimney and enter the chimney after about 30 feet. Climb flakes in the back of the chimney 15 feet, then use opposing force for 15 feet to a roof. Surmount the roof and work back right. The remainder of the route is obvious and finishes with a 6-inch slot.

Electric Fountain Crack. 5.8. First ascent in 1970 by Roger Briggs

and Kristina Solheim. High up and to the right (southwest) of Third Eye is a left-facing dihedral with a partly off-width crack.
Arete. 5.9 (no protection). First ascent in 1984 by Eric Goukas. Just right of Electric Fountain Crack is an arete. Climb its right side.
Solid State. 5.8? First ascent in 1973 by Roger Briggs and Mark Hesse. This is on the rock west of the Achean Pronouncement and offers one pitch with 50 feet of perfect hand-jamming.
Dreadnaught. 5.10. First ascent in 1975 by Scott Woodruff and Dan Hare. On the ridge just west of the Achean Pronouncement is a 200-foot long roof -- the right end of which forms this beautiful dihedral. A rotten pitch leads to the dihedral.
Super Power. 5.11. First ascent in 1980 by Jim Erickson and Roger Briggs. One of Erickson's finest accomplishments, this climbs the impressive crack in the long roof between Solid State and Dreadnaught. The 1st pitch climbs up to a belay below the roof. The 2nd pitch is a climb up the crack past a "pod."

Dinosaur Mountain.

The south, lower summit of Green Mountain, south of Skunk Canyon and north of Bear Canyon has countless routes, for those willing to walk and search. A short distance up the Mallory Cave Trail (which cuts southwest uphill off the Mesa Trail) is found **Square Rock**, a huge boulder that offers difficult top-rope routes on its east face and other challenging routes all around.

Backporch.

The prominent tower of the Backporch is seen south of and above Skunk Canyon, high on the north end of Dinosaur Mountain (the lower southeast knoll of Green Mountain). Follow the Mesa Trail south of Skunk Canyon or approach by hiking west from NCAR.
East Face. 5.5? First ascent in 1956 by Bob Beatty and Bob Jickling. The east face route of the Backporch begins at the northeast corner of the rock. Climb and find a traverse left (north) onto the east face. Work up slabs to the base of a narrow overhang and climb the overhang. Wiggle up to a tree and work up a crack to a belay spot. The next lead goes diagonally right, then left and over another overhang, to a belay point. The summit is then gained by scrambling.
Space-Time Inversion (or the **Five Year Plan**, if done free). 5.13? First ascent in 1971 by Roger and Bill Briggs. Led free in 1985 by

Dale Goddard. This difficult crack (sport-climb) ascends the southwest corner of the Backporch, moving up the impressive crack through an overhang.

East Face of Der Zerkle. 5.7? First ascent in 1972 by Larry Dalke and Pat Ament. This route ascends the east face of the large flatiron directly west of and above Square Rock, on Dinosaur Mountain. Start at the right (north) side of the face. Climb 140 feet to a belay near a tree, below an obvious overhang. Pass the overhang on the right, laybacking a flake, and continue upward to a belay point. The final leads are moderate slabs to the south summit.

Cornucopia. 5.12d or 5.13a. Led free in 1986 by Dale Goddard. This is on the Box -- a ferocious little spire south of and above the backporch. Hike up between the Box and the Finger Flatiron, then north and west until at the Box. Or, as Roger Briggs describes the approach, "Hang a right, high up off the Mallory Cave trail." Cornucopia ascends the center of a concave wall of the upper south side of the Box. Begin from the top of a large boulder. Bolts leads past a hole. A sport-climb, "cheater slings" may be necessary to make clip-ins.

Discipline. 5.12b. Free ascent in 1987 by Hank Caylor and Paul Glover. Begin at the low point of the south face of the Box, about 15 feet right of Cornucopia. Follow bolts up, past a hole, then angle slightly right and through flakes and corners. The first bolt, high off the ground, is sometimes pre-clipped from the side, using a stick.

Rock Atrocity. 5.13d. First ascent led in June 1990 by Colin Lantz. This route is high on Dinosaur Mountain, above Mallory Cave, on the west side of the formation called The Hand. The Hand forms the upper/south boundary of Mallory Cave. The east face of the Hand is a 5.1 climb. Rock Atrocity, however, is up the spectacular west face via a difficult sport-climb.

BEAR MOUNTAIN

South of Green Mountain, this is the pointed summit as seen from central Boulder. The mountain is distinguished by the spire of Devil's Thumb rising on a ridge. Behind Bear to the southwest is South Boulder Peak. The two mountains comprise "Boulder Mountain."

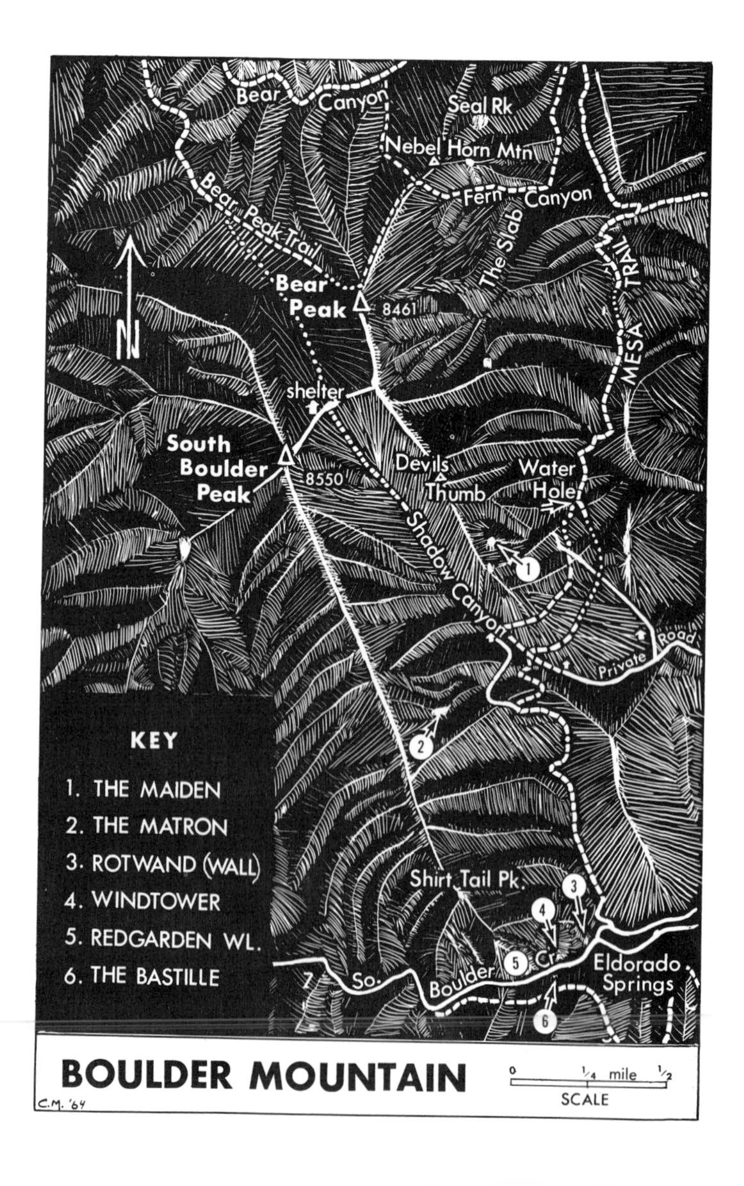

Seal Rock (on the right) and the Goose
photo by Cleve McCarty

The Sanctuary

A top-roping area in Bear Canyon, the approach follows the main trail (under the power lines) to where the first streamlet cuts across the trail. Cut left through the brush for 60-70 feet. The cliff is identified by a blunt arete on the left and a wall extending right. Four top-rope routes were done here in 1986 by Christian Griffith: **Love** (5.12b) is up the left side of a wall (easiest place) to the base of an arete. Step right, onto it, then work straight up. **Fire** (5.12d) starts on the face immediately right of the arete and climbs straight up, making a long reach between two holes. Finish on desperate, thin edges just right of the top of Love. **Variation of Fire** (5.12c) climbs Fire to the first hole (finger bucket) and steps left to Love (above the ramp). Finish up the arete. **Black Streak** (5.12b or c) climbs the obvious black streak right of Fire. There are "lots of pebbles and some holes."

Overhang Rock.

Located south of and above Bear Canyon (the large canyon between Green and Bear Mountains), Overhang Rock is spectacularly formidable on all sides.

Rogue's Arete. 5.10. First ascent in 1963 by Layton Kor and Pat Ament. Directly up the north face of Overhang Rock is this route. A display of Layton Kor's superb free-climbing ability, the route starts on broken ledges and climbs straight up a strenuous dihedral to a belay stance on the right side of the face (just above a tree). Traverse 5 feet left, move diagonally up right a few feet, and make a hard move (5.8+) to the ridge on the right. Continue to a belay stance big enough for a foot or a heel (there is a bolt). The 3rd lead is the cerebral crux. Traverse a short bit left and work diagonally up right, to a prominent flake (or block). Lieback to the top of this flake and climb diagonally right and up, on a vertical wall, to the summit.

To descend, scramble up the ridge crest and make a short rappel south to a saddle from where another longer rappel can be made.

Seal Rock.

The obvious, large flatiron curved like a seal is seen rising above and south of Bear Canyon and north of Fern Canyon. In the late '50s, approach was made from Boulder, via the Mesa Trail, a good pre-climb walk. Now it is easy to approach via NCAR or up Bear Canyon from Table Mesa, getting onto the Mesa Trail in Bear Canyon and wandering south and upward.

South Face. 5.4? First ascent 1959 by Corwin Simmons and Dave Husbands. The first known route to have been done in the Bear Canyon-Fern Canyon area, this crosses the wall and involves ascending an obvious strata that leads up and left. Arrive at a point just west of the summit.

North Face (or **Archaeopteryx**). 5.11+? First done in 1965 as a mixed aid and free-climb by Larry Dalke and Wayne Goss. Climbed free in 1982, following a line that varies somewhat from the original, by Jeff Achey and Roger Briggs. This impressive face, graced by the light of setting sun, had the following initial description: "Climb diagonally left for one lead. Work up to an obvious, yellow band that slants up to the right (west). Strenuous and delicate climbing along the band leads to the notch just west of and below the summit." Roger Briggs recalls about the free ascent, "Jeff's lead of this is surely the most remarkable I've witnessed. The climb as a whole has the exposure and feel of climbing on the Diamond."

Jeff Achey describes the route, "Scramble to a belay point below a somewhat indistinct, left-facing (left-leaning) inside-corner. Pick a line out to the left of the dihedral for 60-70 feet. Move left under an overlap (5.10-). Then climb upward right along a band of rock to a belay at a bolt. This is pretty much the line of the old Dalke-Goss route (it seems?). The 2nd pitch follows a crack up and left. Then surmount the large roof at an apex (5.11) to an exposed belay at two bolts. The 3rd pitch moves left from the belay. Climb generally up and right on an intricate slab (no bolts!) to the summit of Seal Rock. Several 5.10 sections are encountered on this pitch, as well as one of easy 5.11 (20-feet runout)."

The Goose

Immediately south of Seal Rock is this large flatiron. An easy route ascends the right-hand side of the east face. The west face has an interesting one-pitch slab. A number of climbs exist up the south wall (which is part of Fern Canyon).

Sweet & Innocent. 5.10a. First ascent in 1982 by Joel Schiavone and Dan Hare. A fine pitch ascends a small, left-facing corner (with a thin crack) on the steep, west face of the Goose.

Fern Canyon.

Hidden treasures of beauty and climbing are found in this main large valley south of Bear Canyon and Seal Rock. A trail veers southwest off the Mesa Trail, starting near where the Mesa Trail reaches the top of the hill south of Bear Canyon.

Chains Of Love. 5.12b or c. First led in the late 1980's by Colin Lantz. This is a brilliant sport-climb a large roof (or overhang). The route is on the southwest under-side of the second ridge of rock north of the floor of Fern Canyon. Follow the Fern Canyon trail until about at the bottom of the first ridge of rock and take a turn right, uphill in the talus and forest north of the first ridge. Find the huge, bolted overhang.

Ruby Slipper. 5.11. First ascent in 1981 by Jeff Achey and Bill Bradley. Below the south side of the Nebel Horn (the rock spire of the northeast, subsidiary summit of Bear) and located near the top of Fern Canyon, find an elegant, southwest-facing finger-crack up a smooth, red wall.
Violator. 5.13c. First ascent May of 1990 led by Colin Lantz. A 70-foot, beautiful arete is found just right of Ruby Slipper.

The Slab

The long, wide flatiron extending along the bottom east side of Bear Mountain, south of Fern Canyon, is the Slab. Many routes exist, on the northwest side as well as the flatiron-like east face.
North Edge. 5.5? First known ascent in 1977 by Rich Rossiter and Lynn Householder. Take the Fern Canyon trail and cut left to the base of the Slab. Follow small cracks and grooves near the right edge of the huge face. A peculiar ear-like formation hangs in space about 2/3 the way up. Climb behind this and work up to easier terrain.
Keyhole Route. 5.8. First ascent in the early 1980's by Gary Neptune and Jim Glendenning. Spot the route by starting below (under) a type of keyhole formation (a hole behind a couple of giant flakes). The keyhole is the 3rd pitch. To start, climb to scoops and to an overhanging band. Make a delicate mantel up and right (sneak around the band) to a ledge. Then climb upward through the keyhole.

Devil's Thumb

The original Indian name of "Toponas" has been lost to this conspicuous spire of Bear Mountain. The rock has been hitch-hiking for years up the southeast ridge of Bear and still has not caught a ride. In the early days of climbing in Boulder, this rock was an oftensought prize that turned back many an erstwhile climber. The difficulty was encountered midway up the east face at a 15-foot overhang. The problem was later resolved with the addition of a ladder. The ladder no longer exists, but its anchor -- an iron bar -- remains. The approach to the rock is easiest up Shadow Canyon from Eldorado Springs.
Left Side. 5.8. Ascend the left (south) side of the formidable, east overhang.
Right Side. 5.8+. Climb an obvious crack up the right (north) side of the east overhang.

The Maiden.

The slender formation of the Maiden is positioned between two larger flatiron-type rocks, below and south of Devil's Thumb. The rock is known for the spectacular, 115-foot, free rappel from its summit, a rappel first done in 1948 by Brad Vandiver. The exposure on the climbs and traverses give the rock a serious feel, while the rappel from the summit requires expertise in anchoring and in techniques such as keeping ropes from tangling while rappelling. Prudent climbers place the knot that ties the two rappel ropes together below the lip of the overhang before descending. Beginning and intermediate climbers should always be belayed on the rappel.

To quote Cleve McCarty, "In truth, the twisting descent offers an uncontrolled, 360-degree panorama without parallel. During high winds, the rappel takes on a ballistics problem with the bombardier calculating himself as a human bomb while blown well out from the ridge like a pendulum. The target seems no larger than a doormat and is only a point on a ridge, 120 feet from the base of the rock and 115 feet from the top." This point is called the Crow's Nest. Vertical walls drop from either side of it to the ground. Some climbers have camped in the cozy basin at the summit. Cleve McCarty went on a shrimp hunt to this basin with Margaret Powers, complete with nets and bottles, as an errand for the biology department. The trip was a success. There were fresh-water shrimp!

Dale Johnson relates that, in his first days as a beginner, he and equally trained companions attempted the south face several times without ropes! When Baker Armstrong's arm gave out on the rappel, someone had wits enough to tighten the rappel line (against his brake-bar). The summit of any rock is a distinct episode for each individual. The Maiden, like many summits, has changed with the tide of ascents. Roy Holubar writes in a *Trail And Timberline* about an early ascent of the Maiden, "Once on top we marvelled at the size of the place. Two trees and a sheltered, bathtub size depression filled with H20 give the top a very casual, pleasant appearance. The view over the plains with all the vegetation and the many reservoirs is a pleasure. We ate lunch comfortably in the convenient shade of one of the trees." In contrast, William Bassett wrote in 1962, "We arrived together at the airy summit. It was completely bare -- except for cans, bottles, candy bar wrappers, a register, and a sign pointing over the overhang, reading FIRE ESCAPE." The summit continues to be restored to its natural state.

The approach to the Maiden is via the Mesa Trail, coming

north from Eldorado. Take either of the two south alternatives of the Mesa Trail. The now standard trailhead leads upward to forest below and east of the Maiden, while the old Mesa Trail (the start of which is somewhat difficult now to find) begins north of the Eldorado pool and leads up a grassy valley and up Shadow Canyon to a turn uphill back east over talus (aiming left/north of two rock towers). The goal of this approach is the upper west end of the Maiden (an awesome, sudden discovery) and the start of the standard North Face route.

North Face. 5.5 or 5.6? First ascent (for route and summit) October 26, 1944 by Roy Peak and Mark Taggart (see page 4). Taggart was a freshman at Colorado University. Peak was a senior at South High in Denver and made pitons and carabiners in metal shop. These pitons, along with manilla ropes and tennis shoes, were the gear. The descent was made by returning via the ascent route. Taggart recalls, "We didn't know any better."

This popular, exhilarating line climbs down from the upper west end of the rock and traverses east across the north face, via two crux sections, to the east slabs which then are ascended easily. Start with a short wall, get onto the ridge, and descend almost to the Crow's Nest -- the small stopping point for the rappel from the summit. Climb down easy ledges on the north side until confronted by an obvious, smooth wall that separates the easy ledges from another ledge with a tree. This smooth wall is the most difficult section of the climb and is known as "the pendulum pitch." The first ascent party placed a rope here for a "safety pendulum" (that is, they were top-belayed across the section but did not rely heavily on the rope). A few tricky moves allow for a free ascent of this steep slab. From the tree, continue upward east to another good ledge. Two ways exist from here. The first climbs downward to the east and ascends a wall to the left of an inside-corner to a roomy shelf. The second way, the Walton Traverse, ascends diagonally upward and east to a 15-foot, downward traverse that ends at the shelf. This latter (upper) variation is named after Harold Walton, was actually led by his partner Stan Gebura (Walton followed). From the shelf, now moderately easy rock leads up behind a large block, through a notch, and along the east ridge.

Anchors of various sorts have been set for the rappel, but no anchor should be trusted blindly. Some anchors age, and no old sling left by another party should be trusted. It never hurts to sacrifice an extra sling and reinforce a rappel anchor.

Julie Johnson starts the Walton Traverse on the North Face of the Maiden
photo by Cleve McCarty

Northwest Overhang. 5.11? First ascent in 1953 by Dale Johnson, Dave Robertson, and Cary Huston. Free ascent in 1981 by Harrison Dekker and Randy Leavitt. This was the original climbing engagement of the formidable overhang of the Maiden and represented a considerable advance in techniques. Start from the Crow's Nest and ascend (5.9) straight up to a stance. Climb the overhanging headwall past several old bolts and pitons.

West Overhang. 5.11? First ascent in 1956 by Dale Johnson, Phil Robertson, and Cleve McCarty. Free ascent in 1977 by Steve Wunsch and Kevin Bein. From the Crow's Nest, ascend to a stance under the main overhang. "Skirt" the overhang left (5.8). Crawl right, to a belay foothold. A difficult, (5.11) short slot leads upward.

Dale Johnson on the first ascent of the
West Overhang of the Maiden, 1956
photo by Cleve McCarty

Dale Johnson on the West Overhang of the Maiden, 1956 / photo by Cleve McCarty

East Ridge. 5.10+. First ascent in 1953 by Dale Johnson, Phil Robertson, and Cary Huston. Free ascent in 1970 by Steve Wunsch and Diana Hunter. This route has a history of attempt and failure, the scene of struggle between bolters and anti-bolters. A number of early attempts by adventuresome nonbolters were forced back at the overhang. Start roughly 30 feet up along the north side from the lowest point of the rock. Negotiate the first 50 feet by an abrupt lieback of moderate difficulty. Below the ridge proper, the climber is confronted by a 6-foot wall. A thank-heaven hold allows passage to the top of the wall. Belay here in a bowl-like affair. The route now divides briefly into two possibilities. One leads directly around the corner to the east ridge, while the other climbs upward to the right and achieves the ridge near a bolt. Once on the ridge, delicate control over small holds achieves a sloping belay ledge below the prominent overhang. Three bolts allow progress on direct-aid over the obstacle, or free-climb its right-hand (north) edge. The route now traverses up along the south side of the ridge to a conspicuous saddle. Work up smooth slabs to a large overhang and pass it on the right (north) to the shelf at the end of the Walton traverse (see North Face route).

Original Start To East Ridge. 5.4 or 5.5? First ascent in 1952 by George Lamb, David Rose, and Dallas Jackson. Here was the original route during early attempts of the east ridge. Begin about 20 feet up the talus from the regular start. Climb 50 feet up a moderate slab to a point where it tapers and steepens. Traverse left (east) approximately 15 feet and ascend a steep dihedral to a ledge. Work left (east) to the east ridge.

South Face of the Maiden. 5.8. First ascent in 1953 by Harvey Carter and Clifford Smith. Free ascent in 1958 by Gerry Roach and Jeff Wheeler. To find the start of the route, stand out on the talus so that the face can be seen. Near the east ridge is a long crack that curves upward to the right. West of the base of this crack is a talus block against the face. From the talus block, step onto the wall of the south face, go up a few feet, and traverse diagonally left and up. Follow the strata of the rock for one long lead. Now make a slightly delicate traverse around a small corner (bulge) and work up to a ledge below the somewhat prominent hollow near the center of the face. Traverse east, perhaps slightly downward a bit, and find a way up (over a section with small holds) to the east ridge.

The Matron.

South of and above the mouth of Shadow Canyon is the strange, top-heavy rock known as the Matron.

East Ridge. 5.5. First ascent in 1948 by Bill Eubanks, Brad Vandiver, and Stan Black. The 5.5 grading designates the 1st pitch onto the ridge proper, after which the route becomes simpler. Start on the north side of the rock. Climb a short wall and move left to the ridge.

North Face. 5.6. First ascent in 1951 by Karl Gustafson and Skip Green. Walk about 200 feet up along the north side of the rock from the base of the east ridge. Surmount a short chimney formed by a large, leaning slab. A comfortable bench is encountered at the base of the route. The climb unfurls with a nasty lieback in the lower (easterly) of two cracks. Ascend the crack 15 feet and traverse upward to the right (west). Climb daintily into a cave formed by an overhang. Attack the overhang to the right, with a high hold. Continue on course left to a leaning tree and ascend 10 feet, via a crack, to the east ridge.

West Face. 5.8+. First ascent in 1955 by Mike O'Brien, et al. This climbs the imposing west slab on small holds. Near the bottom and on the north flank of the slab are the provocative initials "RKS 1889-1950," suggesting the Matron marks a grave.

South Face. 5.6? First ascent in 1952 by Dale Johnson and Phil Robertson. Hike up along the north side of the Matron and arrive at the base of the west face. Scramble south, down a rocky gully, and turn left (east). Scramble 20 feet to a tree on the south face. Descend a well-defined trough 80 feet to a wide shelf, then traverse 20 feet to a belay point about 10 feet beyond a large boulder. The 2nd lead continues east, with a 30-foot scramble to an eagle's nest. Climb along the southeast side of the nest and follow a crack. Once over this section, work directly over a hump to a marginal belay point. The 4th lead traverses right, to a second eagle's nest, and ascends a smooth (high angle) slab. At the top of the slab, traverse right, on tricky rock, to a thin ridge. Descend this ridge and continue right, on tiny holds, to a small hollow. Belay at this exhilarating stance. Descend slightly from the belay on a traverse around the corner and continue 10 feet to a "glad-one-is-there" stance. This magnificent traverse originally had one bolt for belaying in the hollow but was later subjected to "drillers." Once on the ridge, continue up 30 feet to the only obvious belay point. Follow the north side of the east ridge to the summit.

Other time-honored flatiron climbs and many more obscure ones may be found in Gerry Roach's "Flatiron Classics" guide, published by Fulcrum.

For some nice topos of flatiron rocks, refer to Richard Rossiter's guidebooks.

ELDORADO SPRINGS CANYON

The incredible climbing of Eldorado is found six miles south of Boulder. Drive south on Broadway, leaving Boulder, and watch for the Eldorado turnoff. A daily fee is required to enter, or purchase an annual pass. The area has provided beautiful routes for many generations.

Between 1906 and 1948, aerialist Ivy Baldwin walked his famous tightwire across the canyon. Strung between the summits of the Wind Tower and Bastille (in the earliest days called Chimney Rock), the wire was over three hundred feet high. Notorious Eldorado gusts challenged the balance of the master, yet he walked the wire 89 times. His last crossing was on his 82nd birthday in 1949. He died in the autumn of 1953. The dangers of the wire were many: wind, lightning, blinding sun, and birds.... Getting the wire up in the first place was a feat. It weighed 30,000 pounds. Eighteen guy wires were used. Sacks of sand were added to weight the wire. The first trip across was witnessed by 1500 people. During that first crossing, Ivy stopped in the middle of the wire and stood on his head. He also knelt and lay on his stomach. He regularly wore sunglasses, after once being blinded by the reflection of the sun off the Wind Tower. He sometimes was forced to wait hours in the middle of the wire for the wind to stop. Crossings were made in hailstorms and lightning. He regularly pretended to fall. Ivy, his son Harry, Jack Fowler, and others helped rig the cable. The men started with a small cable, went up the Bastille, and hoisted up the thicker cable. One observation tower was built at the top of the Bastille. Then called Castle Rock (and before that, Chimney Rock), the Bastille had a flight of stairs up its high east face. Five wooden observation "houses" (platforms with roofs) were built at various points along the east side of the Rotwand Wall, one at the top of the Rotwand. The lowest of these houses still exists, frailly. Ivy sometimes practiced by walking the divider ropes in the swimming pool. Toward the end of his career, a smaller wire was strung from the east end of the Rotwand Wall to a crag on the south side (above where the ranger's toll booth now is). This was in part to facilitate onlookers. He encountered strong resistance from his wife prior to his final wire walks. She threatened to shoot the sand out of the weight bags. Unusually high winds attended his last crossing, but at age 82, he knelt in the middle of the wire and waved to 3000 spectators. He was greeted on the other side with a birthday cake.

Early postcard of Ivy Baldwin. The figure on the wire is drawn in almost three times the actual size of a person, and the height of the wire given is 582 feet (actual height is closer to 350 feet)

To quote Bill Fowler, owner of Eldorado for many years, "I can remember back to the '40s when our patrons would go out in tennis shoes and get hung up on the cliffs. You'd get a hunk of lariat rope and go up around back and come down. The earliest fatality was about 1942 when a couple was climbing on that thin, thumb-like spire near Rincon. The boy fell....

"The Colorado-Utah-Southern started a railroad grade in competition with the Moffat railroad. You can see what's left of the old grade behind and at the top of the Bastille. The Moffat line went in about 1500 feet higher, and the Colorado-Utah-Southern was so low and had so many switchbacks that it was a financial disaster. They contracted to individuals for individual miles and got a lot of the easy miles in but didn't get enough of the tough and rockier miles farther up canyon. They started to go broke about at the top of the Bastille. It was an expensive project cutting through that spot. Mr. Neil (who had the ranch up above) made a deal with them to use the grade as a road to his house. During this time, the Barbers and some of the local people were taking milk, eggs, and produce to Central City. This is where their income was derived -- week up and week back.... In 1904, my grandfather, William Garner, and Stockton formed a corporation.... There was a year 'round and good supply of soft, thermal water. Some of this water was even bleeding out of the cliffs. They saw that it was the era of health spas. They... built a 30-room hotel, built a dance hall, and had three different swimming pools. The canyon went as a resort until 1926 when my grandfather, father, and uncle bought up the existing shares.

"The Denver & Interurban ran a spur line up here in the summer. The Craig resort (which was high above Supremacy Slab) had a hotel and burned in 1904 or 1905. Two of the swimming pools were destroyed in the great flood of 1938...."

"A high dive, one of the three big pools"

Rotwand Wall

The first main rock, on the right (north) side of the canyon, this is broken, shattered sandstone of the geologic Lyons formation. The rock is loose and challenging to protect, as well as sharp and pointed -- not a good place to fall (for fear of injuring the body but also of severing the rope). So why mention the rock at all? Strangely the climbing is exhilarating and relatively safe for climbers of the right temperament and ability. Henry Barber, one of the stars of the 1970's, described the route Kinnder Rooten as one of the most intense routes he had done. He was referring to the total concentration and care such climbing arouses in a person. Actually the rock is colorful, lovely at times. An astute climber can usually tell which holds are loose and find protection (with creativity).

The Rotwand Route. 5.8? First ascent in 1960 by Layton Kor and John Auld. Start well left of the east end of the wall, but before the slabby ramp/gully that leads upward to the northwest. Climb an obvious, right-angling (steep) ramp up the main wall to a stance. Now make a long traverse up and left (west) across the nearly vertical wall to a small tree. The 2nd lead weaves a way generally straight up above the tree to the ridge.

Kinnder Rooten. 5.9. First ascent in 1963 by Layton Kor and Pat Ament. The name is Kor's Dutch for "kind of rotten." From the start of the northwest (upward) sloping, slabby gully at the bottom of the wall, scramble up the gully and ascend a short, steep slab in the gully to a kind of hollowed spot. The 1st lead climbs about 30 feet straight up the tricky wall to a tree. Now ascend 60 or so feet directly above the tree to a stance on the left near some blocks, in a band of rock. Step right, move over a roof, move right a bit more, and climb a slab to an obvious roof. Go over the obvious place in the roof or find an easier exit by skirting the roof to the right.

Wind Tower.

The second main rock on the north side of the canyon.

Scotch 'N Soda. 5.11b. First ascent in 1962 by Layton Kor and Charles Roskosz. Free ascent in 1973 by Jim Erickson and Art Higbee. This is a steep, strenuous route up the direct south face of the Wind Tower. The route, in essence, begins atop a "triangle" of rock (two ramps, one slanting upward to the east and the other slanting to the west). From the convergence of the two ramps (the top of the triangle) climb a difficult wall 15 or 20 feet, with protection not easy to get in, and surmount the roof. Above the roof,

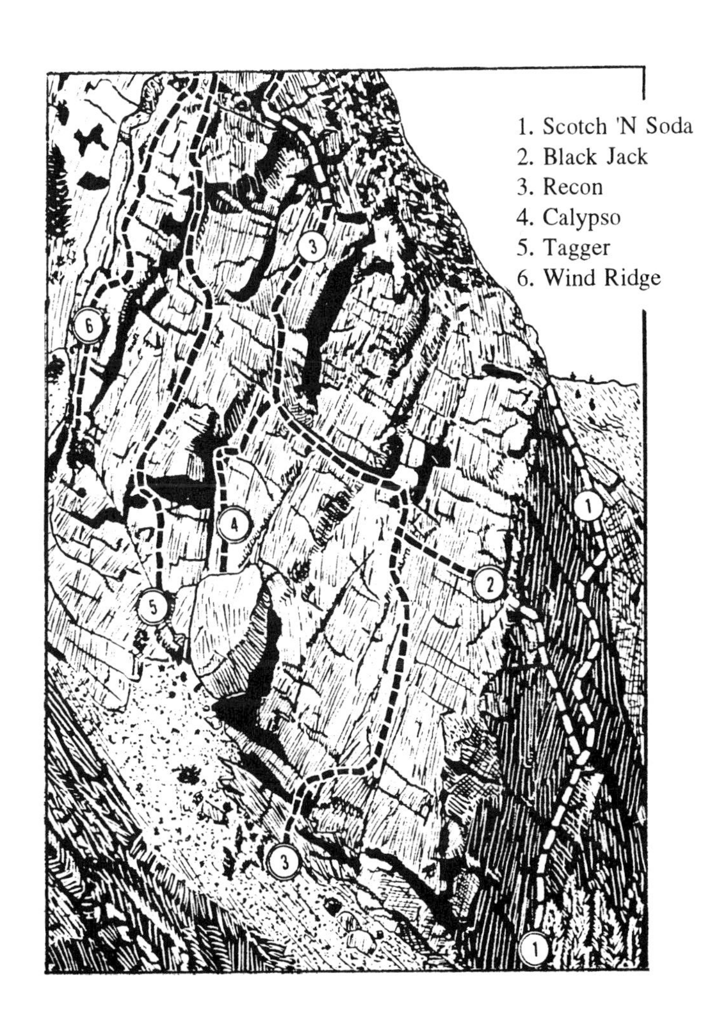
1. Scotch 'N Soda
2. Black Jack
3. Recon
4. Calypso
5. Tagger
6. Wind Ridge
1
2
3
4
5
6

angle up and left a short distance to a belay stance at two bolts. The 2nd lead can be done two ways: One moves up and left, then back right, while the other goes above the belay on more difficult rock. The variations join near a bulge that is climbed. Traverse about 15 feet east to a projection.

Metamorphosis. 5.9+ or 5.10a. First ascent in 1967 by Pat Ament and Gordy Ryan. Free ascent in 1973 by Jim Erickson and Art Higbee. "As Gergor Samska awoke one morning, he found himself transformed into a giant insect." This beautifully vertical route parallels Scotch 'N Soda to the left (west). Approach by climbing part way across the Yellow Traverse (moving 50 feet up and west from the top of the triangle) or scramble easy slabs on the west side of the Wind Tower and move down east along the obvious ledge that angles down the south face of the Wind Tower. Climb into a small, red, left-facing dihedral. Work up the dihedral (stepping briefly out of it to the right and back in). Move steeply up and slightly left, over a bulge, and up sloping, unprotected rock to a small foot-stance to stop and belay. There are two bolts. The next pitch works up and slightly right, with occasional protection. A strenuous pull past a small, hanging flake leads to easier but less protected rock. Creative protection can be found, and eventually a band is reached that leads left and up toward the top.

Disguise. 5.10a or b. First ascent in 1977 by Bill Briggs and Pat Ament. This beautiful, vertical route climbs the upper left (west) side of the south face of the Wind Tower. The easiest approach to the route is up easy slabs on the west side for about 150 feet to the obvious ledge and then down a bit east along the ledge, onto the south side. Climb over a short roof onto the main wall. Ascend steeply and a bit left, then mostly straight up (on slightly fragile holds, with a slightly runout section). Reach a thin crack that arches up and right. Near the start of the crack, step right. Then move up and rejoin the crack. Angle up and right, moving over a weird bulge with down-sloping holds. Steep but easier rock leads upward.

Rainbow Wall. 5.12d or 5.13a? First known ascent, on aid, in 1983 by Kyle Copeland and Mark Hill. Free ascent led in 1984 by Bob Horan (after a few weeks working on it). The free ascent was attempted and nearly obtained by Christian Griffith, Skip Guerin, Chip Ruckgaber, and Harrison Dekker. Bob was accused of stealing the route, since others had done much work to get close. His answer, "To steal it must mean that someone owns it?" The route is one of the most significant of the difficult sport-climbs and marked the age of the 1980's. At the bottom of the south face of the Wind Tower, locate the obvious ramp that slants upward east. Climb this ramp a short distance until below the sheer Rainbow Wall.

King's X. 5.10c. First ascent in 1967 by Layton Kor and Larry Dalke. Free ascent in 1971 by Ron Cox and Paul Sibley. Referred to by Steve Wunsch as "thinking climbing," this classic ascends the right-arching, vertical crack on the lower left (west) edge of the south face of the Wind Tower. Begin a few feet west of a tree and to the right of a big roof. The route can be done in one or two leads, and care must be taken with runners to avoid rope drag. The 1st pitch of the route, for example, can be more difficult for the person who follows than for the leader -- if the leader makes the hard moves and then fails to place protection before traversing left. Start by climbing up flakes to a bulge. Surmount this difficult bulge and move left on much easier rock. An uncomfortable, standing belay may be established up and to the left, or continue up the overlapping layers of rock as it steepens toward an a-shaped apex overhang. The overhang is easier than the rock below the overhang. A belay can be made immediately above the apex, almost in a hang. Or continue higher to a large ledge. From the belay at the apex, an easy traverse is found angling up and left (west) to the simple slabs of the west side (which can crossed north to the talus gully).

The Uplift. 5.10+ (little if any protection). First ascent in 1964 by Pat Ament, Jan Sacherer, and Roger Raubach. Free ascent in 1974 by Duncan Ferguson and John Searls. One of the great and gifted free-climbers of the 1970's, Duncan Ferguson, led this bold, single pitch up the lower southwest corner of the Wind Tower. Start below a roof, surmount the roof around its right side, and ascend a high-angle crease (inset) that slowly peters out. Reach a roof that must be climbed risking a long fall. Exit left onto the easy west-facing slabs.

Calypso. 5.5-5.6. First ascent in 1961 by Layton Kor, Pat Ament, and Larry Dalke. This was Kor's first climb with teenagers Ament and Dalke, done on Thanksgiving Day, a route that has become a classic appealing to thousands of climbers and standing against the wear of time. Begin on the left (north) side of a large boulder sitting at the bottom of the west face of the Wind Tower. Ascend a short chimney-crack, with combined face-climbing techniques, to the top of the boulder. Another start, but not the original, traverses right and across a slab to the top of the boulder. Work diagonally left from the top of the boulder into the obvious, right-facing dihedral. Climb the dihedral to an overhang. Traverse 10 or so feet right, with feet smearing on sloping footholds. Climb over a small bulge and up a thin slab to a belay stance. In later years, two bolts were added to this belay spot, because of the frequent use of the route. From here, a number of choices exist. The classic is Recon, done in 1956 by Dick Bird and Dallas Jackson, up the steep crack directly above the bolts (that route originally started south from the start of Calypso).

Taggar. 5.10b. First ascent in 1962 by Larry Dalke and Pat Ament. Free ascent in 1968 by Jim Erickson. Free ascent in 1968 by Jim Erickson and Jim Walsh. Start just left of the start of Calypso, below a large roof. The 1st pitch of the route climbs the left-curving crack under and through the left (northwest) edge of the roof. This crack is 5.9+, surprisingly moderate for its steepness and yet surprisingly more difficult than it looks. Seventy-five feet up, reach a tree on a ledge to belay. The 2nd lead, much more rarely done than the 1st, goes up moderate rock above the tree and up a right-facing dihedral to a huge roof at the top of the dihedral. The roof is the crux, above which steep, good climbing continues to a large ledge that can be descended to the north. It is important to place runners in such a way as to prevent rope drag over the roof.

Wind Ridge. 5.5-5.6. First ascent in 1959 by Layton Kor and Jane Bendixen. Start near the bottom of the prominent, northwest corner of the Wind Tower. The actual start has caused much confusion, since there are several steep variations -- and none exactly trivial. Either climb a short distance and traverse right (around a corner) and get quickly onto the ridge's southwest slab. Or climb a v-groove and hand-traverse back right, around the corner. Another (slightly more difficult) variation attacks the ridge directly, going up between the two variations. Once on the slab side of the ridge, work up to a roomy, horizontal belay crack. Continue up the ridge and ascend a type of chimney-crack on the right (south) side of a block. From a good belay, surmount a troublesome overhang and climb a steep slab (taking care not to knock loose rock) to a tree. An alternate finish simply descends north along the ledge below the overhang.

Dead On Arrival. 5.11b? Free ascent in 1973 by Jim Erickson and Scott Stewart. This could be Erickson's most impressive achievement, a bold, strenuous pitch up an old aid route located 50-60 feet vertically above the large chockstone in the Redgarden Wall descent gully -- north of the Wind Ridge. The crux climbs the left (south-facing) wall of an overhanging dihedral or roof.

Cinch Crack. 5.12b? Led free in 1978 by John Bragg. This hand/finger-crack through a large roof or overhang is also located near (just above) the big chockstone in the Redgarden Wall descent gully -- north of the Wind Ridge.

The old footbridge, where boards broke and people often fell through. It was part of the Eldorado adventure.

N.E.D. 5.12. First led 1979 by Charlie Fowler (top-roped originally by two climbers from Southern Illinois, names not known). Free-soloed in the mid-1980's by Bob Horan. This is the large roof above the northeast end of the cement platform (at the southwest corner of the Whale's Tail).

The Bastille.

Once called Chimney Rock, this is the obvious, 300-foot tower on the left (south) side of Eldorado Canyon.

Werk Supp. 5.9+. First ascent (with one point of aid) in 1964 by Ralph Warsfield and Pat Ament. Free ascent in 1964 by Dave Rearick and Pat Ament. This route ascends the lower left (east) portion of the Bastille's north face. Start about 40 feet east along the road from the Bastille Crack and just right (west) of an obvious, blocky dihedral. Climb straight up and, after about 20 feet, make a strenuous move left and up. Make a step or two up right. Now stay on the steep hand/finger-crack with face-holds up the elegant wall.

Peter Croft climbing solo on Werk Supp / photo by Pat Ament

One rope-length of climbing ends at a good, easterly-slanting ledge with two bolts (added years later because of the popularity of the route). Scramble left into a kind of trough and down (east) a short distance to the start of a conspicuous, right-slanting jam-lieback crack in a wall. This is the crux and finishes at a ledge.

Last Pitch Of March Of Dimes. 5.10a or b. First ascent in 1973 by Dudley Chelton and Duncan Ferguson. This is a nice direct finish to Werk Supp or can be approached after climbing two pitches of the Bastille Crack. The lower pitches of March Of Dimes are not that interesting. From the shelf (ledge) at the top of the right-leaning jam crack (the 2nd pitch of Werk Supp), this left-angling finger-crack pierces a vertical wall. The crack leads to an exit left, below a small roof, from where a belay can be established. Descend to the east, down a slabby ramp, with trees.

The Bastille Crack. 5.7+ or 5.8. First ascent in 1954 or 1955 by two U.S. Army climbers. The route was later climbed free. Stan Shepard relates some ancient history:

"Allen Bergen and I were walking down the road our first visit to Eldorado in 1957. Allen, what does this thing remind you of? Uh, it looks like a castle, he replied, but we can't call it that. There must be a thousand Castle Rocks in Colorado already... I've got it, the Bastille, how does that sound? Maybe. Allen led the first free ascent of the 2nd pitch of the crack a week later. I did the first lead via the so-called Northcutt Start. After making the first few moves free, I used aid. Allen led the 2nd and 3rd leads entirely without protection (this was his first real rock climb) and scared me to death. On the upper part of the route, he pulled some loose blocks onto himself and received bruises and a shaking. So, one lead from the top, we retreated."

Start atop some broken ledges at the bottom middle of the north face of the Bastille. Climb about 15 feet to a stance inside a large, thin, protruding flake. Step left (west) onto a slippery hold, reach left, and lean over into a hand-jam or lieback crack that is climbed to a good belay stance with two bolts (approximately 60 feet above the ground). This 1st pitch is the crux and has been the site of a number of serious leader falls where people have hit the ground. Intermediate climbers should be careful to place sufficient protection and make sure it is the kind that won't fall out as the leader passes it. The 2nd lead continues up the obvious crack about 90 feet, moving left near the top of the pitch as the crack juts right.

-- Pat Ament, age 14 (early 1960's), leads the Bastille Crack
photo by Cleve McCarty

A good belay is found. This pitch is known for its pigeons which sometimes fly unexpectedly out of the crack. The 3rd lead continues 35 or 40 feet up a steep wall to a belay on a sloping ledge. The 4th lead is longer and wiggles up a large, broken, inside-corner system starting at the back of the sloping ledge and angling slightly left at first. Eventually a big, sloping ramp affords a belay. The final lead ascends broken rock to an easy chimney (left crack of two).

Variation to Finish. 5.8. First ascent in 1959 by Layton Kor and Dave Dornan. At the end of the 4th lead of the Bastille Crack, move up right, along the big ramp, and ascend a steep, left-facing dihedral via a slightly off-width crack (done as an off-width or a lieback).

Northcutt Start. 5.10d or 5.11a. First led free in 1959 by Ray Northcutt. This was done after Northcutt was falsely informed that the route had been climbed by Layton Kor. The route is a direct start, or rather an alternative 1st pitch, to the Bastille Crack. It was the original aid start by Stan Shepard in 1957. Find the crack a short distance left (east) of the normal 1st pitch. Where the crack diminishes, a strenuous finger-traverse moves up and around the corner to the right. Immediately around the corner, work straight up to the bolts.

Derek Hersey on Northcutt Start / photo by Steve Gay --

Outer Space. 5.10a. First ascent in 1961 by Layton Kor and Steve Komito. Free ascent of 1st lead in 1971 by Jim Erickson and Pat Ament. Free ascent of 2nd lead in 1971 by Jim Erickson and Diana Hunter. Start by climbing two pitches of the Bastille Crack.

Now traverse upward and right (west) along sloping rock, around a small corner, and move up the left side of an inset slab. Aim for the obvious red dihedral above. Move up to and out of a small alcove at the start of the dihedral. These moves and the first move into the dihedral are the most difficult on the climb. At the top of the dihedral, scramble right and up along the obvious broken band as the band becomes a good ledge. Belay here, before reaching the west side. The 2nd pitch is one of the most spectacular in the canyon and ascends the middle of the headwall of the upper north face of the Bastille. The beautiful, vertical crack up the headwall must be obtained by traversing from the belay ledge outward and upward (to the east), across friable flakes and rock somewhat tricky to protect.

Wide Country. 5.10d or 5.11a? First ascent in 1967 by Roger Briggs and Neal Foster. First pitch led free in 1972 by Jim Erickson. Free ascent in 1972 by Duncan Ferguson and Don Peterson. Start almost at the same place as the start of the Bastille Crack, just a bit to the right. Work up 70 feet (5.8+ or 5.9 and not too well protected) to a bolt. Traverse left across a steep wall (moving slightly upward), to a mantel onto a sloping hold. Continue left a bit, then up toward a down-hanging flake that points the way back up and right. At the end of the traverse up and right, climb the last easy part of the 2nd pitch of X-M to a belay stance. From here, find a thin traverse left -- going almost to the Bastille Crack (this traverse is the technical crux). Above, head straight up a couple of difficult, short inside-corners (crossing the 1st pitch of Outer Space). From a belay spot, the final lead ascends the impressive northeast corner of the huge summit block (upper fifth, and tricky protection).

X-M. 5.10c. First ascent in 1962 by Layton Kor and Pat Ament. Led free in 1967 by Larry Dalke (with Cliff Jennings). Start a step or two right of Wide Country. The original route climbed the wall to the left of the obvious crack-chimney (the chimney formed by the left side of the huge pillar on the northwest corner of the Bastille). The free ascent followed the chimney instead of the wall to the left, but later, in 1968, the wall to the left (distinguished by a steep finger/hand-crack) was free-climbed by Ron Cox and John Behrens. The left wall is the more interesting, and at the top of the finger/hand-crack is an interesting traverse right -- into the chimney above where the chimney is difficult. Belay near the top of the chimney, inside the chimney on a foothold or on top of the pillar. The 2nd pitch 5.10c moves out of the chimney (to the east) and ascends two or three body lengths up a shallow, left-facing inside-corner. Make a wide step left to a foothold and easier rock that goes up to a belay stance. Ament remembers, "At the start of the 2nd pitch, I leaned left and hammered in a tiny R.U.R.P. but was hesitant to stand up on it. I asked Layton if the thing would hold. He said he would test it for me. We switched positions. With me on belay, he attached his aid-sling to the R.U.R.P. and stood up onto the tiny piton without hammering at it or re-placing it. 'See it holds,' he said."

Kor placed a bolt on the 2nd pitch, well out left and after the thin section. Another minor bolt war errupted here in the late '80s when a climber removed that bolt and re-placed it lower -- to protect the free moves out of the chimney. The new bolt was removed. Now no bolt at all exists. But none really is necessary, and people with a creative understanding of natural gear protection are able to find ways to protect the lead.

The 3rd pitch has two variations. The original route goes up and right (via an undercling flake), then face-climbs a few moves to a hand-traverse left. The other variation angles up and slightly left and, with a scary move, joins the other route at the end of the hand-traverse. The pitch continues up another few body lengths to a belay point. The 4th pitch climbs toward the dihedral of the 1st pitch of Outer Space, then soon traverses right (west) and up across a steep, bulging wall, around a corner, to a left-facing dihedral that is ascended to the large ledge below the headwall of Outer Space. It is possible now to join the last pitch of Outer Space or move around the corner to the west and ascend easy rock to the summit.

Northwest Corner of the Bastille. 5.11-. First ascent in 1959 by Layton Kor and Peter Lev. Led free in 1966 by Pat Ament. At the bottom of the northwest corner, about where the west side talus begins, climb left across a slab below a small roof. Move up and right, along obvious strata a few feet, then up and left via a flake that is more or less hand-traversed. Stand onto the flake which is now a small ledge. Ascend a steep, difficult (5.9) wall, moving a bit right, toward a protruding hold. From a good stance, ascend an obvious, moderate crack to a two-bolt belay stance in the crack behind the huge pillar on the northwest corner. The 2nd lead is the crux. Jam and lieback up a dihedral (first free climbed in 1964 by Dave Rearick). Climb a short, difficult overhang (5.9) to a rest foothold on the left. Ascend straight up the red headwall via a thin crack (the original aid route) and reach up right for the famous, hidden mantel-hold which the leader must mantel or face-climb past. On the free ascent, Ament began aiding from the rest foothold but suddenly spotted the mantel-hold and realized the route would go free. Without feeling a need to unclip his rope from the three pitons in the crack, he lowered to where he had stopped free-climbing and started up again to make the moves free.

Once standing on the mantel-hold, the climbing is easier (still 5.9-) up a recessed wall below an overhang. Traverse right a move or two and get onto a beautifully exposed stance out on the corner of the rock.

Instead of reaching for the mantel-shelf, one may also continue up the crack (finding a finger-hold out on the wall to the left of the crack). Move right, to step onto the mantel-shelf. This slightly more difficult variation, done first by Pat Ament in the '70s, will feel more protected and is a beautiful, airy example of Eldorado climbing on vertical rock with exposure. The rest of the climb (two more pitches to easy rock) stays on the corner, or it is possible from the top of the 2nd pitch to traverse right (south), around a corner, and up a bit, to reach ledges that can be traverse-descended to the talus gully on the west side of the Bastille. Stan Shepard recalls, "Rick Horn and I did the first... and I recommend it to be the last... midnight, foul weather winter ascent of this route after being propagandized by Rebuffat's film, *Starlight And Storm.* The idea was mine, but Rick did all the work, leading storm-lashed rock by scratting along on fingernails and knees. I fell, almost fell, didn't quite fall, repeatedly while seconding. I thought the material of his wet knicker knees had a greater affinity to the rock than did mine. In retrospect, note that it was, in reality, his tremendous skill that got us off the ground."

A young Roger Briggs belays Pat Ament,
on the first ascent of Northwest Corner, 1966,
photo by Pat Ament

Rain. 5.10d (protection not as good as a leader would like). First ascent in 1967 by Pat Ament and Tom Ruwitch in a severe downpour to test newly purchased cagoules. Free ascent in 1975 by David Breashears and Ajax Greene. Start a few feet up the slope along the west side from the start of the Northwest Corner. Work straight up steep rock, then move left under a type of roof (using underclings). Climb over the left side of the little roof and work right, to a bolt. The two bolts placed on the first ascent were short, thin, experimental bolts not designed to be fallen on. Bolts have since been added, eliminating some of the scariness. The route goes up the vertical, gray rock and will be discovered. It connects eventually with the Northwest Corner or, if you like, West Buttress.
West Buttress of the Bastille. 5.9+. First ascent in 1959 by Layton Kor and Carl Pfiffner. Free ascent in 1964 by Layton Kor and Larry Dalke. This outstanding route begins up along the west side of the Bastille, just below the huge talus block. Climb about 5 feet up a small, right-facing inside-corner, move around the corner left (north), and hand-traverse 10 feet left to a thin, vertical finger-crack. Ascend the finger-crack about two body lengths and make a long step left to easier rock. Ascending the finger-crack directly, without stepping left, is more difficult (5.10a) but worthwhile because of its elegant rock. The two variations converge about 15 or 20 feet higher, as the pitch continues up steep, enjoyable rock to a two-bolt belay. The 2nd pitch goes up the obvious crack formed by the left (north) side of a huge, protruding flake. This crack, nearly as difficult as the 1st pitch (extremely difficult if you are not adept at crack climbing), involves a rounded lieback into a chimney. The 3rd lead, 5.7+, works left along broken rock to an overhang with a wide crack. Above the overhang, a narrow wall just left of the crack offers good holds.
Hair City. 5.9+. First ascent 1969 by John Behrens, Stan Badgett, and Jim Erickson. Starting at the same place as the West Buttress of the Bastille, climb a small, right-facing inside-corner. Mantel onto a balance shelf. Get standing on the shelf and move right. Originally, this traverse right did not go all the way to the protection cracks (of the West Face route) and ended by making a scary move up to a bolt (placed by rappel prior to the ascent). Continue left, onto a kind of corner, and work up thin rock to a 2nd bolt. Follow steep rock, mostly straight up, to the lower outer face of the huge flake of the West Buttress. Traverse left across the flake and reach its (upper) left edge. Face-climbing leads to the top of the flake.

This is a long lead. The 2nd pitch ascends the impressive overhang above (5.9+), directly between the two obvious cracks, and works up a classic wall on good holds to a ledge. Fourth-class rock remains.

Christian Griffith solo on West Buttress / photo by Dan Corrigan

West Face of the Bastille. 5.9+ or 5.10a. First ascent in 1961 by Bob Culp and Stan Shepard. Free ascent in 1968 by John Behrens and Jim Erickson. Start between the main wall and large talus boulder, a few steps up to the right of the start of the West Buttress route. This is the steep finger-crack system leading upward (slightly right). The route is reached by traversing in from the right or by a difficult, short finger-crack (5.10). About 40 feet above the ground, where the rock becomes a bulge, move left 10 or 15 feet. Reach a bolt and continue straight up. A more difficult finish, instead of traversing 10 or 15 feet left, is to continue up the crack (5.11a).
Blind Faith. 5.9+. First ascent in 1972 free-solo by Jim Erickson. A short walk uphill south (perhaps 200 feet) from the start of the West Buttress of the Bastille, look for a vertical hand-crack that goes up a gradually steepening wall and up the left side of an overhanging block. This is the route, with an optional 5.9 2nd pitch (or traverse carefully south down a ledge and off, after the 1st pitch).
Neon Lights. 5.10d. First ascent in 1975 by Art Higbee, Jim Erickson, John Ruger, and Ed Webster. High up along the west side of the Bastille, past some trees, and not far below the old road, is a 30-foot crack. Work up this, then up a steep wall 40 feet. Belay on a small ledge. Continue up 100 or so feet to the descent ledge from the summit of the Bastille. The 3rd pitch is the steep, interesting crux, a right-angling hand-crack up an overhanging wall. From the top, descend north into a gully to an easy down-climb back to the ledge. The 3rd pitch of this route is often done as a climb all in itself, approaching from the Bastille descent ledge or after climbing another Bastille route.
Your Mother. 5.12d. First ascent in 1988 by Colin Lantz and Greg Robinson. This sport-climb ascends the bolted west-facing overhang left (north) of Neon Lights. The climb distinguishes itself as where the Bosch power drill was used in Eldorado for the first time. Colin was proud to have the first drill in town. To place the bolts, the rock was too overhanging to allow for a simple rappel. Colin reverse-aided the overhang, starting from the top and working downward with nuts, cams, hooks..., and placing the bolts as he went.

Redgarden Wall.

This is the largest rock in Eldorado Canyon, rising in its wide, multi-colored, sunlit way on the north side of the river. Pigeons glide serenely past edges of the wall, adding to a sense of the rock's height.

The Bulge. 5.7+ or 5.8. First ascent in 1957 by Layton Kor and Ben Chidlaw. No bolts were placed on this route during the first ascent, but bolts have since been added to several belay spots. The bolt on the crux bulge of the 3rd pitch was added by Kor soon after the first ascent, on the request of area climbers who considered the route too dangerous. This is one of the best routes in Eldorado, a high-angle climb on good holds. Start well up into the east side of the bushy couloir between the Whale's Tail and Redgarden Wall. Begin with a steep, unprotected slab. Reach a short headwall that is passed by moving up and right (starting from a sloping, protruding stone). Proceed up pocketed rock to a belay stance on footholds under an overhang. The route continues up and right, on the wall beneath (and east of) the overhang, for about 20 or 25 feet. From a stance, follow the natural strata of the rock diagonally left and up (runout) to a belay with bolts on sloping footholds. The 3rd pitch angles up and slightly right, about 25 feet. Find a protection bolt and move left and over the bulge from which the route got its name. Above the bulge, it is possible to find protection to prevent the second climber from swinging in the event the second falls. Move over a small overhang a short distance above the bulge and follow the natural, left-angling crease of the rock to a belay spot. The final pitch ascends diagonally right, ending on easy slabs. To descend, cross the easy slabs in an upward fashion to the north, walk north up a grassy trough, and down-climb a short, northeast-facing dihedral with a tree. Hike east and then south down the gully.

Derek Hersey begins up the first pitch of the Bulge
photo by Pat Ament

Black Walk. 5.10a. First ascent in 1963 by Layton Kor and T.J. Boggs. Free ascent in 1971 by Jim and Dave Erickson. This route follows a steep line up the east side of the imposing, water-blackened wall left (west) of the Bulge. Climb 20 feet, up an easy slab, move over a small lip to the right, and meet the steep wall. Angle up and left 15 or 20 feet, along a kind of steep ramp, to a bolt. The remainder of the pitch goes more or less straight up the very steep (vertical) wall, the crux coming quickly above another bolt. After a runout, a belay stance is reached where there are bolts from which to rappel. Or find the 2nd pitch which goes up and left about 20 feet, with a 5.8 or 5.9 move getting onto a foothold near a bolt. Work right, under an overhang, on thin holds. Easier slabs lead to the top.

Back Talk. 5.11-. First ascent in 1986 by Todd Montgomery and Darius Azin. This route goes up the steep wall just to the right of Black Walk. Start the same as Black Walk. Start up the steep, left-angling ramp at the beginning of Black Walk and, from just above a poorly located bolt, work across a steep wall to the right. Hand traverse back up and left on vertical rock to another bolt. From here, go straight up to a two-bolt belay. The crux, for a leader, is the end of the half-rope-length pitch, where the holds get rounded and greasy and protection is scary.

Pseudo Sidetrack. 5.4. First ascent in 1958 by Stan Shepard and Don Davis. Shepard recalls, "Don and I thought we had done Sidetrack, until someone told us we had not." This is perhaps the easiest route up Redgarden Wall, always climbing on good holds and weaving upward first west and then east, with occasional airy sections. It should not be considered a beginner's climb, since there are traverses a fall from which might cause a second person to pendulum or drop below and over steeper rock. Start near the west end of the grassy platform that is the top (highest part) of the couloir between the Whale's Tail and Redgarden Wall. Climb 40 or so feet upward along a black ramp, move around a corner (hanging slabs) to the left, and continue upward west to a good stance for a belay. The 2nd pitch continues in the same direction, upward and west, aiming for a line that passes above an obvious roof. Past the roof and above, find a stance to belay or run the rope out higher. The 3rd lead reaches a large ledge above with a tree. Now the route heads upward and east, following an obvious inside-corner, then moving around some bulges to a ledge. The final lead goes up a steep wall on good holds to trees. Scramble north to the descent.

The Whistle Stop. 5.8+. First ascent in 1958 by Tom Quinn and David Jones. Walk north up along the west side of the Whale's Tail and scramble east a bit up into the couloir (rocky gully) between the Whale's Tail and Redgarden Wall. The route starts near the third lowest chockstone in the couloir. A short, tricky wall puts the climber onto a ramp that slants upward left to a sloping belay. Above, climb steep rock up, then left, to a finger crack that angles slightly upward right on a sleek face. As the crack thins, continue up and diagonally right, over an overhang, toward Pseudo Sidetrack.
Direct Variation. 5.9. Where the finger-crack diminishes on the 2nd pitch of Whistle Stop, continue straight up (slightly left), passing two bolts, to the right end of an overhang. Move left to a belay (pitons at a horizontal crack, under the overhang).
The Flakes. 5.8. First ascent in 1961 by Pat Ament and Larry Dalke. Free ascent in 1970 by Duncan Ferguson, Bill Conklin, Dave Clark, and Jim Erickson. A good short pitch to Whistle Stop. Near the bottom west entrance to the couloir between Whale's Tail and Redgarden Wall, find a left-facing dihedral that juts left in steps.
Slab Variation. 5.9. First known ascent led by Pat Ament (in the '70s?). From the top of the 1st pitch of Whistle Stop, traverse right and out onto a steep slab. Ascend the slab via a thin flake (or seam).
C'est La Vie. 5.11b or c. First ascent in 1962 by Pat Ament and Jeff Wheeler, (using only one or two pitons for aid in the dihedral). Led free in 1973 by Bob Williams. Ament recalls the first attempt on this route (1961 or '62) when Larry Dalke experienced an acute appendicitis 50 feet up the 1st lead. From the cement platform near the river, walk directly north up the talus and scramble onto a ledge to start. Ascend approximately 50 feet, following a small inset up a wall, to a bolt. This bolt was added in recent times, whereas the original bolt (used for years) was poorly placed, half-way in, several feet lower. On the first ascent, the lieback of the obvious flake above was a formidable proposition -- no chalk, no sticky rubber shoes, and a small bolt sticking half out of the wall far below. Getting to the lieback flake and into the lieback position is perhaps the crux of this pitch, now lacking some of the former mental challenge but every bit as difficult. A belay from two bolts is found just above the lieback flake, under a left-leaning roof. A leader may wish to combine this pitch with the next, since both pitches together are less than a rope length, but this midway belay allows for better communication. The 2nd pitch (or second half of 1st) goes over an a-shaped overhang (a step right), then traverses left to a good belay

stance under the huge overhang. The large, right-slanting dihedral above is the crux. At its top, traverse right, along broken rock below a roof, to a foothold belay. A descent can be effected by a traverse downward east, a full rope-length (following the easiest strata), into the grassy couloir.

Desdichado. 5.13c or d? First ascent led in 1986 by Christian Griffith. The most spectacular sport-climb in Colorado, this route crosses west out and under the huge roof above the C'est La Vie Dihedral. Pre-placed bolts (no easy task) allow for a "siege" line of sensational position. Begin the route just after completing the hardest moves of the C'est La Vie dihedral.

Genesis. 5.12c. First ascent in 1962 by Jack Turner and Bob Culp. Led free in 1979 by Jim Collins. This aid-climb was originally done using R.U.R.P.s, tiny Chouinard pitons. The cracks eventually enlarged, from the piton usage of various ascents, opening the crack to fingertips. Start to the left of C'est La Vie, at the base of a broken, red dihedral that slants upward slightly to the left.

Jim Collins leads the free ascent
of Genesis, 1979
-- photo by Pat Ament

Climb the dihedral (first moderate, then 5.9). Angle left over a strenuous bulge, with a step left to a rest foothold at the bottom of the classic, red slab. The remainder of the route is obvious, ascending upward right, climbing a thin flake vertically to its top, and ascending the crux headwall to the roof above -- from where a traverse right leads to easier rock.

Lakme. 5.13b. First ascent led in 1987 by Christian Griffith. Start up Genesis. Above the initial difficult bulge of the 1st pitch of that route and near the start of the thin flake, move up and right -- to bolts on the amazing arete.

Anthill Direct. 5.8. First ascent in 1961 by Layton Kor and Rick Tidrick. First pitch done in 1958 by Harvey Carter and Sheldon Schargart. Start about 50 feet west along the base of the wall from C'est La Vie, east of a group of trees. Ascend up and slightly left,

along a narrow, black-washed ramp. After about 60 feet or so, work left 15 feet and move up and around a difficult bulge (feet above a roof) with marginal protection. Ascend diagonally left and slightly up, then straight up, to a belay stance at the bottom east end of the "Lower Meadow" (the slanting, grassy ledge a quarter of the way up Redgarden Wall). From here, the route goes over an obvious, exposed overhang (not too difficult). Climb diagonally left, on moderate slabs about 60 feet, to a belay stance at the base of a short, left-facing dihedral (the dihedral leads about 20 feet up to a roof). Work up to and over the roof (5.7+ or 5.8 hand-crack). Traverse well left, moving diagonally upward, passing a delicate move or two, and ascend a steep finger-crack that slants up and slightly right. Traverse 15 or so feet left to a narrow shelf. Now ascend a groove that slants up and right. From a horizontal indentation, surmount a bulge and climb a steep slab on an exposed corner. A belay will be found above, from where it is possible to traverse left and go up.

Redguard Route. 5.8. First ascent in 1956 by Dick Bird, Chuck Merley, Cary Huston, Dale Johnson, and Dallas Jackson. This was one of the first routes in Eldorado, a historical piece worth doing. Start behind a group of trees, left (west) of the start of Anthill Direct (roughly a hundred feet west of the start of C'est La Vie). The 1st lead, named "the Birdwalk" after its pioneer Dick Bird, is the most difficult of the climb, although one may find an anxious moment on the last (led by Chuck Merley). Just west of the easternmost tree, work up 15 feet to a ledge. Traverse left on sloping, tricky rock for 15-20 feet to the start of a 20-foot crack that runs upward through two bulges. One may also climb the obvious rock straight up to this crack, as a direct start, and there is another variation between the two previously mentioned.

Ascend the vertical, bulging crack beginning where the three variations converge and traverse 15-20 feet left onto a large shelf. The 2nd lead ascends the easterly of two cracks and works up (and slightly left) on steep, broken rock to the Lower Meadow (the big, slanting ledge). Scramble up the meadow to a tree near a roof. Climb the lip east of the tree (slightly lower) and work up easy rock for 25 feet or so to a belay roost (hole). Begin the 3rd pitch with a short lieback to a large dihedral. The left slab of the dihedral is a black-washed ramp that is climbed (or lieback directly up the dihedral) until it is possible to make a foot-traverse 5 feet left to a narrow belay stance. The 4th lead continues 140 feet up the tapering ramp-dihedral to a bi-level hole. The 5th lead climbs 140 feet up a series of slightly rotten grooves to a small, shallow cave (or hole). The last pitch starts a little below the east lip of the cave. Ascend straight up a steep face to a narrow ledge. To finish, scramble north up a prominent trough and pass a huge block on its left side. Easy descent is found down slabs to the northeast.

Larry Dalke beginning the middle variation of Birdwalk, 1961 -- photo by Pat Ament

Diving Board. 5.10+ or 5.11. First ascent in 1962 by Layton Kor and Larry Dalke. Free ascent in 1972 by Roger Briggs and Jim Erickson. In the mid-'70s, "hot" Henry Barber demonstrated his mental control when, on the 2nd pitch of this route, he dislocated his shoulder and managed to hang upside-down, put his shoulder back in place, and extricate himself from the situation.

Henry Barber in about 1976 / photo by Pat Ament

Climb Redguard Route to the bi-level hole. Follow the next lead of Redguard 60 feet or so to a stance in a black groove. Work up and diagonally left, across a slab, to a sloping belay stance at the base of the overpowering wall above. Climb straight up a dihedral and ascend the left side of the "pigeon flake." From the top of the flake, move left (west) and step across a wide, tricky gap. Ascend a steep, slightly rotten band of rock to a long, overhanging inside-corner (5.10). Belay at the "black hole." The final lead liebacks right and follows a chimney (left side in) to a jam-crack that later presents a short, off-width section (the crux).

The Naked Edge. 5.11b. First ascent in 1962 by Layton Kor and Bob Culp. Direct finish completed in 1964 by Kor and Rick Horn. Free ascent in 1971 by Jim Erickson and Duncan Ferguson. First pitch done free in 1971 by Steve Wunsch. Final hand-jam of the 4th pitch led free in 1966 by Larry Dalke. Stan Shepard and Bob Boucher were the first to try this route, venturing up the unexplored initial pitch and into the domain of Eldorado's beautiful sandstone. Perhaps the most obvious line in Eldorado, this route was a focus of early pioneers of climbing and later became a focus for free-climbing in the early '70s. Singular position and continuousness create a route of superb interest, a line admired but also mocked. It has been done nude, also in drag (by Mark Wilford and companion).

Jim Collins free-soloed the route in the mid-'70s, and Derek Hersey free-soloed it in 1984. Hersey free-soloed it several more times after that. The route remains a serious, splendorous, undertaking.

Layton Kor, 2nd pitch of Naked Edge -- photo by Pat Ament

Climb two pitches of Redguard Route and continue up the grassy Lower Meadow (or approach by other routes). Climbers have used Touch 'N Go as a start, or Kloeberdanz, or the Wisdom, as examples. In any case, reach the small ledge at the base of the Edge. If the approach is made up from the Lower Meadow, climb and lieback out an obvious cave at the top of the meadow to the start ledge. The 1st pitch (5.10d or perhaps 5.11a) is 70 feet long and goes up a steep, thin, finger-crack above the ledge to a belay stance with two bolts. The original aid line now went right, up, then left beneath the obvious overhang. This variation was done free in 1974 by Bob Candelaria and David Breashears. Jim Logan recalls attempting this variation and having his rope untie. He watched in horror as the rope slid down through the carabiners. He was able to down-climb the gear and retrieve the rope. The now standard 2nd pitch goes up the edge-face above the belay. Both variations join at the left edge of the large overhang, where a steep crack in a wall is followed (5.10) to a belay shelf. The 3rd lead, with a 5.8 mantel as its crux, stays near the obvious arete. The remainder of the route goes out the overhanging corner in two pitches: face-climbing, hanging out of a slot, an undercling, liebacks, hand-cracks.... The 4th pitch, often thought the crux of the climb, once was a bold, frightening pitch, altered through the years by the addition of pitons.

4th pitch of the Naked Edge / photo by Bob Godfrey

Touch 'N Go. 5.8+ or 5.9-. First ascent in 1966 by Pat Ament and Gary Spitzer. Most definitely a classic that has survived the test of time, this may be the most frequently ascended route on Redgarden Wall and continues to attract climbers of all abilities.

From the start of Redguard Route, walk west and around the corner uphill for about 60 feet. Start below the lower right end of a small, left-slanting roof. Step onto the rock below the roof. Traverse left, under the roof. Where it ends, make a strenuous move upward (5.8). Get onto a stance atop a flake, below two small dihedrals that face each other and converge a short distance above. Climb this enjoyable formation and continue up the finger/hand-crack above to a good belay at the obvious, angling crack-ledge. Now traverse left (west) and upward a short bit to the start of a classic, right-facing, right-leaning dihedral. This is the crux, a series of continuous moves progressively more difficult. Eventually the Lower Meadow is reached, as are two large eye-bolts placed in recent years.

T-2. 5.10b. First ascent in 1959 by Layton Kor and Gerry Roach. Free ascent in 1962 by Dave Rearick and Bob Culp. This is one of the finest routes in the canyon and one of the first major free routes in Eldorado.

Originally it began after climbing two pitches of Redguard. Soon after, Kor did the lower wall with Charles Roskosz. The beginning surmounted the overhang near its right end, standing atop of a talus boulder and reaching a bolt at the lip. Aid was used to get onto the wall, and then a free traverse went left (west) across the wall to where vertical rock was ascended free over a small roof to a belay ledge. The free ascent surmounted the overhang near its left end, below the left end of the traverse, after a bolt was placed by rappel. This variation started atop a talus spike standing out of the talus. The spike has long since fallen over, and a good horn to wrap fingers around broke off, but other holds allow for a direct (slightly more difficult) start off the ground from deeper under the overhang. The bolt for this variation was later replaced by a piton driven into a drilled hole.

Begin uphill and west of the start of Touch 'N Go, at a point under an overhang where a slab of flat rock comes out of the ground and begins to angle upward west toward a tree. Ascend the overhang, the crux of the route, and work up vertical, enjoyable rock to a roof that is climbed. A belay point is reached half a rope length above. Traverse 20 feet left (west) from the belay and work up into a shallow chimney. Where the chimney ends, climb a short inside-corner and find a belay stance in a crack (or higher, on a pedestal). The 3rd pitch works diagonally left and up a rotten, red jam-crack. Traverse left, around a corner, to the lowest end of the Upper Meadow. Walk about 70 feet west up the meadow to begin the 4th lead. Ascend 60 feet vertically where there is a recess in the wall. From a stance at the base of a black-washed gully, make a tricky balance traverse left 15 or 20 feet across a vertical, yellow wall. Ascend a prominent (slightly left-angling), vertical finger-crack (5.9) up an aesthetic wall for about 50 feet to a narrow belay shelf. Continue diagonally up and left, along the crack as it widens. Reach a prominent ramp that slants upward to the right. Climb 90 feet up along the top (inside) edge of the ramp to a belay spot below a distinct, red overhang. The next lead is short (5.9) and climbs up and left across the overhang. Belay on a good ledge, after which the route finishes by climbing several hundred feet diagonally left (west) on ledges and moderate rock to the large saddle between Tower 1 and Tower 2 (T-2).

Jules Verne. 5.11 (protection difficult). First ascent in 1967 by Pat Ament and Larry Dalke. First lead done free in 1971 by Bill Putnam. Fourth and 6th pitches done free in 1975 by Steve Wunsch and Jim Erickson. First continuous ascent (from the ground) in 1976 or '77 by Roger Briggs and Bob Candelaria. Jules Verne said that one could do anything, if it could be imagined. Start very near the start of T-2. Avoid the original R.U.R.P. crack of Jules Verne (several R.U.R.P.s were used, plus a hook, to aid the overhang), and climb the overhang (using a few of the T-2 holds). At the lip, move left. Free-climb to a narrow overhang that slants up and left. Work up under this overhang and eventually move over it to the right (near its top). Climb a 5.9 slab to a belay stance. Ascend the vertical wall above, using a thin flake that bends first right and then left. Stem up between a short inside-corner and a bulge to the left. Belay in a hole-like affair. The 3rd pitch follows a well-defined, left-angling crack to the lowest (east) end of the Upper Meadow. Just left (west) of the Naked Edge, work right and then left, above the meadow, to a remarkable little pillar. Ascend a narrow, right-facing inside-corner that slants up and left to a tiny roof. Follow a line of small holds on unprotected rock (just left of the original aid flake). One may wish to set small wires or crack 'n ups in the old aid flake. Reach a band of broken rock. Traverse left about 40 feet, along the band, past a 5.8 move. Climb 10 feet to a sloping belay point.

Ascend directly up vertical rock, traverse right (on a narrow ledge), and climb straight up to a belay stance at the bottom of some low-angle rock. Work straight up to a distinct overhang (a type of roof). Ascend a difficult crack in the overhang (5.10) to a belay on a steep wall. From here, climb 150 feet straight up steep, tricky rock to the top.

Lene's Dream. 5.11 (protection difficult). First ascent in 1976 by Roger Briggs and Scott Woodruff. This variation veers off, above the 4th pitch of Jules Verne. After the crux of Jules Verne, at the finish of the unprotected section of the 4th pitch, go straight up (instead of traversing left). This blank-looking wall is ascended to the end of the 2nd pitch of the Naked Edge.

Kloeberdanz. 5.11a or 5.11c (depending on body size and reach. First ascent in 1963 by Layton Kor and Larry Dalke. Free ascent in 1974 by Steve Wunsch and Jim Erickson. Kor worked as a bricklayer for the Kloeberdanz Construction Company. In Bob Godfrey's history *"CLIMB!"*, Bob Culp relates that Kor sometimes tied the rope to himself in those days with some kind of enormous knot he made up. On Kor's first inspection of this route with Culp, Layton led up, leaned out on a piton, and it pulled. He fell, was caught by a lower piton, and his large, balled-up tie-in knot hit him in the stomach and made him ill for quite a time. Wunsch's ascent was with a huge, dynamic lunge. The route was climbed in 1975 statically, on-sight, by a young David Breashears, whereupon he earned the name "The Kloeberdanz Kid." An impetuous, young Breashears ambled up the slope and offered a few suggestions to Roger Briggs who, above, was working at the crux. Briggs answered, "Maybe you'd like to come up and try it." David did and succeeded.

Start near a tree uphill left (west) of the start of T-2. Climb a 5.8+ wall (slightly rotten) to the big ceiling overhead. Move out right, over the ceiling, to a wall under another huge roof. Traverse steep rock east (under the huge roof) to a belay foothold near the right (east) edge of the higher roof. Continue right and ascend a prominent black streak (5.9+ or more). Move left to a belay stance with a bolt. The next lead, first done free in 1965 by Larry Dalke and Wayne Goss, moves 20 feet left (west) on small holds and works straight up 25 feet via a 5.9+ finger-tip crack difficult to protect. Climb a short, moderate overhang, move left, and run out the rope to the Upper Meadow.

White Lies. 5.13? Free ascent led in 1987 by Bob Candelaria. Led as a "red-point" in 1988 by Jim Karn (red-point is the sport-climber's term for leading, with no taints, although not necessarily doing such a lead on-sight). This route starts with the Kloeberdanz roof, then moves out left -- spectacularly. The route above will be found, up and right -- toward the top of the 2nd pitch of Kloeberdanz!

Guenese. 5.11. First ascent in 1962 by Layton Kor and Ron Foreman. Free ascent in 1972 by Steve Wunsch, Jim Erickson, and Scott Stewart. Start about 15 or 20 feet left of the tree near Kloeberdanz. Work up the wall, angling slightly right, to a bolt, traverse 7 feet right, get onto a small stance, and go straight up with tricky protection to the roof where small, strenuous finger-holds along the crack under the roof lead left 10 or 15 feet. Bolts have been added at the end of this traverse which substantially decrease the difficulty of having to hang and set protection, the original crux of the climb -- eliminated. Now surmount the roof. From the lip of the roof, ascend the obvious dihedral above to a belay foothold about half way up the dihedral (or a little more). Move left, around a corner, out of the dihedral. Traverse well left (west), surmount a short headwall on its left side, and work up easier rock diagonally right. From a narrow belay stance, work up a short wall, enter a gully on the right, and follow the gully until it is natural to veer off right and attain the Upper Meadow.

The dihedral of Guenese was climbed all the way up in 1977 by David Breashears and Kevin Worral (probably 5.11).

Psycho. 5.12c. First ascent in 1962 by Layton Kor and Huntley Ingalls. Led free in 1975 by Steve Wunsch. First pitch led free in 1974 by Jim Erickson and Art Higbee. After a hold on the roof broke and made the route slightly more difficult, the route was led in the later '70s by Jim Collins. Start about a hundred feet left (west) along the base of the wall from the start of Kloeberdanz. Climb 15 feet up rotten rock. Follow a thin crack (a type of small, steep ramp) up and slightly left. Make a tricky move up and right. Eventually reach a bolt and traverse straight right, to a belay (hanging) beneath the big ceiling. Surmount the ceiling with bolts for protection. Belay (virtually hanging) in a small, right-arching inside-corner. The next lead (the original 2nd pitch) moves left along the lip of the roof. Reach a bolt (placed by the second ascent party on the insistence of Kor who did a bold, unprotected lead and regretted not finding a place to stop to place a bolt). From the bolt, move upward slightly right (one still risks a bad fall below the roof, with the bolt).

Continue up and left into a shallow, steep dihedral. Approximately half way up the dihedral, traverse 20 feet or so right, surmount a short slab, and traverse up and left to a belay stance near a small, rotten hole. This belay is just west of an eye-catching, smooth slab that is the final lead. Traverse east, clip a bolt, and make a series of delicate moves (5.9) up the slab diagonally right.

Temporary Like Achilles. 5.13c? First ascent in 1967 by Pat Ament and Larry Dalke. Free ascent of first pitch in 1974 by Steve Wunsch and John Bragg. Free ascent of roof led in 1991 by Ben Moon. Start about 20 feet left of the start of Psycho and go up the vertical wall to the roof which is climbed. Christian Griffith envisioned climbing this and replaced one of the old bolts and added another, before inviting Moon to try the climb. The name is the title of a Bob Dylan song with the lyric, "kneeling 'neath your ceiling, honey why are you so hard?" Ben Moon proposed a new name for the route: **Undertaker**.

The Wisdom. 5.11+? First ascent in 1962 by Layton Kor and Pat Ament, a morning after much snow had fallen. Led free in 1978 by John Bachar. First lead done free in 1975 by Ed Webster, Roger Briggs, Jim Erickson, and Art Higbee. The main roof was led free in 1975 by Bob Candelaria who took a spectacular fall through space when a hold broke at the lip. Begin about 40 feet up the Lower Ramp, near the highest end of a long, downward-angling tongue of rock. Work straight up the vertical wall to a rotten band of rock. Traverse around a corner to the right, get onto a little stance, and lieback up a right-facing inside-corner. Belay in a large, cozy cave below the huge ceiling. On the first ascent, the route began up and left of the start here described and reached the rotten band higher. A traverse downward to the east was involved, on loose holds, with no protection for the second man.

The 2nd lead is one of the most spectacular in the canyon and heads out diagonally right, under the roof. The free line, a bit different from the original aid line, heads downward (east) along the lip of the roof and across vertical rock, passing an optional, although unnecessary bolt belay (established by early free attempts). The old aid route went directly up from the lip, over a small roof, up a steep wall to a belay in slings, then right and up to a right-facing dihedral. The free line stays lower, below that small roof. The original aid line above the main roof was done free (5.12) in 1985 by Christian Griffith and Dale Goddard and named **St. Eve**.

Higher Wisdom (or Scary Canary). 5.12. First ascent in 1979 (rope solo) by Roger Briggs. Free ascent in 1980 by Roger and Bill Briggs. From the belay cave below the Wisdom roof, start up the Wisdom roof. Where Wisdom traverses right, under the roof, continue up and left in the obvious, awesome, airy dihedral. Well up into the dihedral, surmount the roof (move out at a pin, on flakes) to bolts and a 5.10+ headwall (diagonally left).

Roger Briggs / photo by Pat Ament

Love Minus Zero. 5.11? First ascent in 1967 by Pat Ament and Tom Ruwitch. Free ascent in 1975 by David Breashears, Art Higbee, and John Ruger. First pitch done free in 1973 by Jim Erickson, Chris Reveley, and Art Higbee. Starting on the Upper Meadow, just left of the start of the 4th pitch of T-2, move 15 feet diagonally up and right, then follow a faint crack system diagonally up and left on a steep, yellow wall. Eventually make a short traverse left to a small, narrow belay shelf. From here, ascend a short, narrow, left-facing inside-corner. This section was done free in 1973 by Roger and Bill Briggs. The route now attacks the right (east) end of a prominent roof. Follow cracks above to a belay point and easier rock to the top.

Le Void. 5.11+? First ascent in 1963 by Larry Dalke and Pat Ament. Free ascent in 1981 by Jeff Achey and Roger Briggs. Free ascent of 1st pitch in 1976 by Steve Wunsch. Ament brought some homemade R.U.R.P.s to try, the soft metal of which turned to mush with a single blow from his hammer. This was the beginning of "bashies." On the roof, Dalke stood on a knife-blade piton that pulled under the weight of much lighter Ament. The two succeeding at the climb, and safely back at the base, Dalke tripped over a talus boulder and broke his leg. Ament carried him down on his shoulders. One of those days.

On the Upper Meadow, left of the start of the 4th pitch of T-2, are two left-facing inside-corners that lead up toward a large, prominent roof. Climb either dihedral (the left is the original line, and right was done free in 1977 by Art Higbee). From a stance below an overhanging wall, climb 20 feet up an overhanging crack and belay (almost hanging) at the base of a rotten dihedral. The 2nd lead works up the dihedral and surmounts the strenuous roof. Climb a vertical wall 40 feet to a belay stance. Two moderate pitches work diagonally left and attain the saddle between towers 1 and 2.

Rosy Crucifixion. 5.10a. First ascent in 1962 by Layton Kor and Jack Turner. Free ascent in 1970 by Jim Erickson, Steve Wood, and Ed Wright. Scramble to the top of the Lower Ramp. From the tree against the main wall, scramble east through (and down) a gap (chimney). Angle right, across exposed, easy rock to a ledge that slants down and east. The route begins where the ledge tapers and ends. Traverse east, about 40 feet across a vertical wall with exhilarating exposure. The first 15 feet are the most difficult and, before a bolt was added in recent times, were somewhat daring. These first moves, prior to the addition of the bolt, clearly determined if a climber belonged on the route or not. Without a bolt, it was required of the leader to rise rather immediately to the measure of the difficulties (or return later after more preparation). At the end of the traverse, either establish a belay on a foothold (may help to prevent rope drag) or continue up the vertical wall via a hand/finger-crack to a better belay shelf. The final lead continues up the steep crack for about 25 feet to where it is possible to do a short, tricky traverse right (5.9), to another crack that leads upward.

Ruper. 5.8. First ascent in 1961 by Layton Kor and Bob Culp. First half of the route done in 1961 by Kor and Ed Risley. This is a superb route legendary for its lovely, exposed 2nd pitch and the slippery crack of the 1st pitch that has repulsed many a climber while trapping the knee of a few others. As with Rosy Crucifixion, scramble to the top of the Lower Ramp. From the tree close to the wall, go east through the gap (chimney), scramble right (over exposed but easy rock) to the slanting ledge, and climb west up the slanting ledge (in spring and summer, beware of poison

-- Bob Culp on Rosy Crucifixion -- photo by Jane Culp

ivy). From the upper end of this slanting ledge (or ramp), ascend a short wall to a small belay area at a block of rock. The 1st pitch begins here. Traverse about 20 feet right (east), on sloping rock, and ascend the notorious Ruper Crack. Above the crack, find a good belay ledge. The 2nd pitch, the Ruper Traverse, follows an exhilarating path right (east), in and out of a couple small dihedrals, then down and right with a wide step (over empty spaces) to a small, left-facing inside-corner that points the way to a tree on the Upper Ramp. To get to the start of the next pitch, scramble down and northeast across the Upper Ramp to the west end of the Upper Meadow, just below and right of the huge cave. Ascend a vertical, left-facing inside-corner 15 or 20 feet. Move left, out onto the steep wall, and ascend (slightly diagonally left, relatively unprotected) about 60 feet. Angle back right and reach a belay stance atop an obvious flake. The next pitch leads straight up the obvious inside-corner to a cramped belay stance below a large, red overhang. The final pitch is the crux and a bit unprotected. Move left and edge up a difficult slab to some bucket holds beneath the overhang. Hand-traverse left, carefully past a loose block, to easier rock.

The Grand Giraffe. 5.10a or b. First ascent in 1960 by Layton Kor and George Hurley. Free ascent made a short time after by Bob Culp and George Hurley. The crux of this route, an off-width crack through an overhang, was originally done by stepping on a piton and perhaps grabbing another. Culp remembers that to eliminate those small aids was probably no more difficult. This route was at the top of the standard for its day, in terms of free-climbing. The route, originally rated 5.8, then a few years later 5.9, is finally 5.10. This is in part due to a small escalation of gradings over the years but also because flakes that served as handholds inside the crack have broken off year after year -- leaving the crack smooth and formidable. Asked what route he would take to heaven with him if he could bring only one, Bob Culp answered, "For whatever reason, probably the Grand Giraffe." In 1969, Culp completed his 50th ascent of the route. Start by climbing to the top of the Lower Ramp. Close to the main wall is a large tree above which is the 1st pitch. Move up to a large flake that must be surmounted gingerly with a move left. Work up to a belay in an alcove at the bottom of a large

Bob Culp leading the 2nd pitch of Grand Giraffe
-- photo by Bob Godfrey

left-facing dihedral (the dihedral of Rover). A more difficult start follows a steep, shallow, right-facing dihedral (5.9), moving up steep rock and slightly right -- to the belay alcove. From the alcove, move diagonally up and left on a steep face with a crack. The first part of this steep face can be done directly up the crack (more difficult) or by moving up and right, onto a flake, and (after a move upward) stepping back left to the crack. The crack (now finger-hand size) is followed to a nice belay shelf. The 3rd lead continues upward along the obvious, slightly left-angling crack system (which opens wider, like a chimney, part way up). Exiting out of the wide part of the crack, a short, tricky, right-facing dihedral leads to a small belay shelf at the base of the formidable crux off-width (the 4th pitch). Above the overhang, on the spacious Upper Ramp, scramble east, down the north side of the huge ramp, to the upper west end of the huge cave (of Exhibit A). Ascend steep, lovely rock for about 90 feet, angling very slightly to the right, and find a narrow stance to belay. The final pitch begins with a steep traverse diagonally upward left on a red, pocketed wall. After about 20 feet, the route ascends a rib of rock, moving slightly upward to the right. Good holds become abundant now to the large saddle at the top.

Super Slab. 5.10b or c? First ascent in 1961 by Layton Kor and Rick Horn. Free ascent in 1967 by Pat Ament, Richard Smith, and Tom Ruwitch. Begin about 40 feet west, up a ledge, from the tree (close to the wall) at the top of the Lower Ramp. Climb 30 feet up a smooth, vertical face (with an obvious undercling flake), past a 5.10 move. Continue up steep rock to a traverse left (west) and slightly downward, using brittle-looking flakes. The final moves of the traverse go up and onto a small shelf at the bottom of a left-facing dihedral. The 2nd pitch climbs the dihedral to a ledge. The 3rd pitch is a bit elusive. Climb about 15 feet above the belay, move a few feet diagonally left, go up a tiny left-facing inside-corner for 5 or so feet, and traverse left around a blind corner (5.8+) to the bottom of an exposed, colorful, and classic "super slab." Climb about 30 feet up the center of the slab to a good, lovely belay shelf. From the west end of the stance, work straight up thin cracks and flakes for about 20 feet (a newly placed bolt protects this formerly runout section. Continue up a shallow, left-facing inside-corner that slants slightly right. Move upward left to a final headwall that is ascended with a move up and right.

Redgarden Wall, South Face

The Doub/Griffith Route. 5.11a? First ascent in 1981 by Eric Doub and Christian Griffith. First pitch done in 1981 by Eric Doub and Eric Goukas. Although the bolts were placed by rappel, this was a respectable achievement for two climbers ages 15 and 16. The humble name for the route must be attributed to youth. From the start of Super Slab, traverse upward west along the crack-ledge and around onto the sunset side of the wall. Find a steep pitch that begins with a small overhang. Work up a short crack. Traverse about 10 feet right, to an arete that is climbed. Step right, to the belay at the end of the 1st pitch of Super Slab. Climb the moderate, left-facing dihedral that is the 2nd pitch of Super Slab. From the belay, move down and left about 10 feet and ascend straight up to the bottom of the classic Super Slab. Work left from the Super Slab belay and follow the left (west) margin of the slab (teetering on the actual arete higher up).

A variation, done in 1985 by Jeff Achey and Dan Stone, eliminates all use of the Super Slab route. Work straight up and over a roof on the 1st pitch and then right (up an arete) on the 2nd pitch.

E.L. (English Language) 100. 5.7? First ascent in 1966 by George Hurley and Gary Spitzer. This is a beginning course in serious climbing. Start near the top of the Upper Ramp, just west of a large chimney (the Chockstone Chimney). Climb a big tree that grows near the wall and, as the branches of the tree fall away, grab the wall. Work up and right, to good holds. Zig-zag up to a prominent crack that leads up the steep face. Where the angle of the wall lessens, this crack becomes an easy open book. At the top of this is an excellent ledge. Go east along the ledge about 15 feet and climb the wall about 20 feet. Follow a right-slanting crack until the angle eases. Ascend, going up and left, on big face-holds, and follow a ridge to the summit of the Yellow Spur (Tower 1).

Vertigo. 5.11b. First ascent in 1961 by Dave Dornan and Pete Lev. Free ascent in 1966 by Pat Ament and Roger Briggs. Second pitch done free in 1963 by Dave Rearick and Pat Ament. About the 1966 free ascent of the route, Ament recalls, "I wore a pair of mountain boots Cub Schaefer gave me to try out on rock. I used a stretchy Columbian nylon rope I didn't trust. I was belayed by a 14-year-old kid I wasn't sure could catch me. I had no chalk. I had to hammer in the pitons climbers have the benefit now of clipping, and I led the 5.11 move first try. Dalke had told me he'd done the upper section of the dihedral free and that it wasn't much harder than 5.8. So when I got the difficult moves, and as my assorted adversities wore me out, I gave myself the benefit of the doubt that I could -- under normal circumstances -- lead 5.8. I took one or two short rests, a hand on a carabiner...."

Vertigo is one of the outstanding free-climbs in the Boulder area and ascends a conspicuous, red dihedral that is part of an obvious, left-angling crack system piercing the right side of the lower, southerly west face of Redgarden Wall (around the corner west from Super Slab). Approach from the tree atop the Lower Ramp. Walk west along the ledge from the tree. Where the ledge becomes an exposed crack, climb (rope is advised) left and up along the broken rock. Eventually arrive around the corner at a big ledge on the west side of Redgarden Wall. It also is possible to approach this ledge by walking up the talus west of Redgarden Wall and (from near the start of the Yellow Spur) walking south along the ledge. The 1st pitch can be done either of two ways. One variation works diagonally up and right, around a corner, and climbs a dihedral (5.9) that slants up and left. The obvious, easier alternative climbs a 5.6 crack left (north) of the dihedral. Both variations arrive at a ledge. The 2nd pitch (led free in 1963 by Dave Rearick) continues up difficult rock (5.9+ or 5.10-), through a type of shallow slot. Above this, follow moderate rock toward the bottom of the formidable dihedral. Find a belay shelf on the right wall, below the dihedral. The 3rd lead climbs the dihedral. Exit left to a nice, sitting belay. The 4th pitch scrambles easily north about 20 feet, under the big overhang, to a crack that goes ten feet up the left (north) end of the overhang. At the top of this crack, walk back right (south), with feet on the upper lip of the overhang. Surmount a short wall and angle up and left along an easy crack.

Vertigo Direct. 5.10+. First ascent in 1973 by Henry Barber and John Stannard. Capable of climbing much more difficult rock than this, Stannard was disturbed by the prospect of falling and swinging far out into free space. So he prusiked the pitch, coming second. This is the airy, overhanging, hugely exposed roof above the Vertigo dihedral. A good crack goes through the roof, and the climbing is more reasonable than the steepness allows anyone to imagine could be the case.

The Yellow Spur. 5.9. First ascent in 1959 by Layton Kor and Dave Dornan. Free ascent in 1964 by Royal Robbins and Pat Ament. Bolt ladder at top led free in 1967 by Larry Dalke.

Royal Robbins writes about the Yellow Spur in the September 1964 issue of *Summit Magazine*, "One moves delicately upward on small holds, with the rock falling away steeply below. One here can experience some of the finest beauties rock climbing offers." Walk north up the talus west of Redgarden Wall, passing west along an obvious, large talus block. Above and north of the talus block, scramble up slabs. The route starts from the highest of a series of ledges, near the northernmost of a group of trees.

Starting off a stone on the ledge, climb straight up the cracks near the tree to the left (north) end of an overhang. Either climb the overhang directly (easier, because of a huge, hidden hold) or ascend the vertical wall to its left (done by Robbins and Ament on the free ascent). Reach a narrow ledge. Walk right (south) along the ledge and work up to a belay tree. From the tree, traverse 15 or 20 feet left (north) and upward to the base of a steep, right-facing inside-corner. Climb straight up the inside-corner and move up and right, to a horizontal cleft (or crack). Traverse left (north) along this to a belay ledge. The 3rd pitch goes straight up, with one 5.7 move, to a rotten ledge. Climb a short, difficult overhang and into an insecure dihedral that leads to a belay ledge. The 4th pitch is easy and moves right, along the ledge, then up into a huge dihedral that ends below a large roof (or overhang). The 5th lead begins with an elegant hand-traverse right and up, below the roof. Ascend a short inside-corner to a shelf on the left. Work up another short inside-corner 15 feet and move right, to an exposed belay stance on a tiny, airy ledge. Lead six climbs straight up a vertical, yellow wall, passing some of the old, early pitons. Below a bolt ladder (the original aid route), move left (and slightly up) across the steep wall. This traverse was first done in 1963 by Dave Rearick and Pat Ament. Attain the obvious arete above which provides a small but good belay stance. The final pitch follows the knife-edge arete to the pointed summit of the Yellow Spur where there is a wonderful view in all directions.

The Green Spur. 5.9+ or 5.10a. First ascent in 1960 by Dave Dornan and Dallas Jackson. Free ascent led in 1964 by Larry Dalke. One of the finest routes in the canyon begins just uphill north a short distance from the Yellow Spur and beyond (north of) the obvious chimney-gully of the Dirty Deed route. Start in a short, west-facing inside-corner. Climb this 10 feet to a flat ledge. Continue a short distance up the inside-corner above to a belay ledge at the base of a jam-crack. Now climb 40 or 50 feet up the jam-crack (just left of a prominent inside-corner). Ascend a difficult (5.9+ or 5.10a), right-facing dihedral that slants up and slightly

Pointed summit of the Yellow Spur
-- photo by Cleve McCarty

right. Before the top of the dihedral, step right and ascend a small, straight-up crease to a belay stance. A short, easy lead ends on a large belay ledge above. Scramble up the ledge (north) and behind (under) a huge block (or around it left) to a tree. The next lead goes 40 feet up an inside-corner on the right, ascends a wall (almost an overhang) and works up a V-shaped trough (or gully) to a belay ledge with a tree. From here, scramble up the continuation of the trough and, from a tree, traverse around a corner left. Now work up an easy inside-corner to the summit. Descend by scrambling north and then west down a high-angle gully.

Grandmother's Challenge. 5.10a or b. First ascent in 1963 by Layton Kor, Pat Ament, and Deane Moore. Free ascent in 1968 by Jim Erickson and John Behrens. Just left of Green Spur is an impressive jam-crack (facing south) that leads to a large, red overhang. Climb the jam-crack (5.8+) to a small belay stance below the overhang. The crux ascends the awkward crack in the overhang, with a slightly less difficult undercling-lieback over the lip. Find a small foothold for belaying above the overhang. The 3rd pitch is straightforward, directly up the slightly rotten wall to a big ledge.

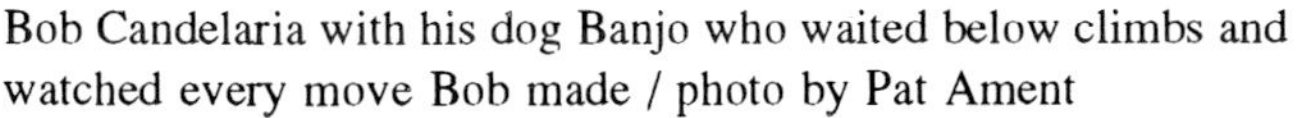

Bob Candelaria with his dog Banjo who waited below climbs and watched every move Bob made / photo by Pat Ament

1. Lower Grand Giraffe
2. Upper Grand Giraffe
3. Super Slab
4. Vertigo
5. Mickey Mouse Nailup
6. Pigeon Crack
7. Exit Stage Left
8. Yellow Spur
9. Green Spur
10. Grandmother's Challenge
11. Green Slab
12. Hot Spur

Paris Girl. 5.12+. First ascent in 1985 (top-rope, later led) by Christian Griffith. This is a 140-foot, imposing, blank wall found a short walk uphill to the north from the start of Grandmother's Challenge. Rappel-placed bolts allow for a difficult sport-climb.

The West Ridge.

This is the prominent outcrop-ridge of rock running north and south, immediately west of Redgarden Wall. The west-facing wall has many short routes of beautiful quality.

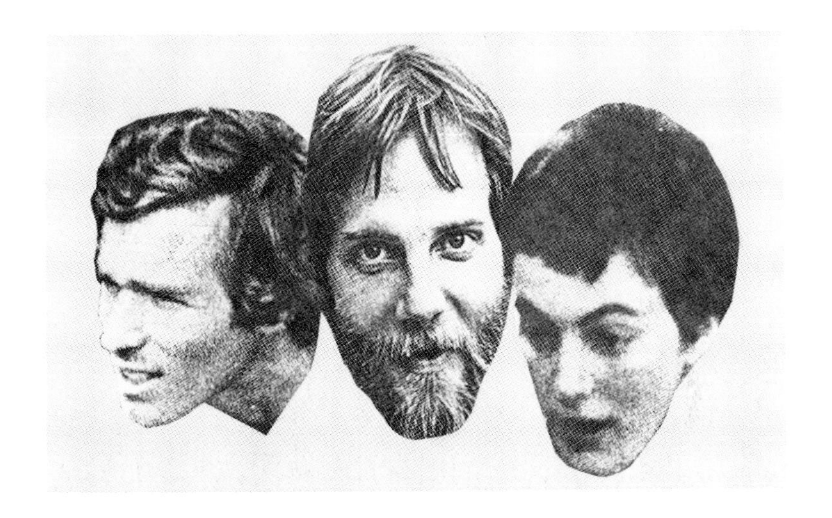

Three of the stars of the 1970's,
Duncan Ferguson, Steve Wunsch, and Diana Hunter

Morning Thunder. 5.9+. First ascent in 1979 by Pat Ament and Christian Griffith. A couple hundred feet above the river is a small, flat, south-face of a rectangular block. The face has a thin crack zig-zagging up through it, starting at the lower left edge of the face and ending at the upper right. This 60-foot route is a lovely example of the exquisite climbing and colorful, sunlit sandstone of the West Ridge.

Blues Power. 5.12a? First ascent in 1981 by Skip Guerin and Bob Horan. Near the bottom of the West Ridge, on a large ledge above the ground, and in a huge alcove/overhang above the top of Morning Thunder, is a hand-crack slanting left through the impressive overhang.

Office Girls Walk The Plank. 5.12. Led free in 1986 by Charlie Fowler. A few inches right of Blues Power (and a few inches left of the overhanging slot of Wing Shot), climb an imposing, thin crack.

Charlie Fowler
-- photo by Pat Ament

Cruisin' For Burgers. 5.10b or c. First ascent in 1975 by Bob Candelaria, Jim Erickson, and Pat Ament. A couple hundred yards up the west side from the river is a shallow, right-facing dihedral seen up on the wall just at the right edge of a roof. The 1st lead starts on a ledge near a tree. Climb to the right side of a large, detached flake (not seen from below but suddenly discovered). Carefully ascend the flake to its top and climb the beautiful, shallow dihedral above. Reach a belay stance on a broken band of rock. Either scramble up a crack left to a rappel tree or do an optional 2nd pitch (5.9) that moves right a bit, up a short difficult section, left a bit, and straight to the top.

Break On Through. 5.10a. First ascent in 1968 by Jim Erickson and John Behrens. Walk up the slopes north from the start of Cruisin For Burgers. Look for the first, most obvious, right-facing dihedral. This is Washington Irving, a 5.6 climb. Just left of the start of Washington Irving, starting on a ledge 20 feet above the ground, lieback a right-facing dihedral (5.8) and follow cracks to a good belay stance on a large, easy slab at a tree. Scramble up to the overhang above and ascend a tight, classic dihedral through it.

Long John Wall. 5.8. First ascent in 1964 (using two or three points of aid on the initial overhang) by Larry Dalke, Pat Ament, and Wayne Goss. Free ascent in 1966 (bypassing the overhang to the left) by Pat Ament and Dean Juhan. This is the longest and one of the finest routes on the West Ridge. Hike up the talus slope past the start of Washington Irving and Break On Through. Start near a large tree, at the base of an easy slab that leads 35 feet to a large overhang. The first ascent party used a small bit of aid to climb the overhang (which later went free at 5.10, in 1973, by Bob Candelaria). The following description incorporates the Ament-Juhan variation that bypasses the overhang to the left.

Scramble up the slab and follow a ledge-like rib of rock diagonally left. Ascend a short wall and traverse right (south) to a point above the overhang. Climb a moderate slab to a belay ledge below a 50-foot, vertical wall. Ascend the wall to a ledge below a small roof (overhang). Climb the left (north) end of the roof and follow a moderate slab to a rotten, red band of rock where a belay can be made. Traverse 30 or so feet left (north) along the band and ascend a 30-foot slot. Once out of the slot, follow easy rock for about 20 feet to a belay point at the top of a huge flake (or block). The 4th lead is the most difficult and ascends the left-hand dihedral of two, up through a large inset, to a ledge. The final pitch goes straight up a wide recess (dihedral-chimney).

Incarnation. 5.13a. First ascent led in 1987 by Bob Horan. A bolted route up the steep, south wall of the Long John Wall tower (on the sheer south side of the tower). Approach from the east.

French Fry. 5.12c. First ascent in 1987 by Bob Horan and Pat Adams. A bolted route up the south wall of the crispy Potato Chip formation north along the skyline from the Long John Wall summit.

Side Wall. 5.11a or b (protection taxing). First ascent in 1966 by Pat Ament and Roger Briggs. Free ascent in 1974 by Jim Erickson, Steve Wunsch, and John Bragg. First continuous lead in 1975 by David Breashears. From the start of Long John Wall, walk up the talus slope north approximately 100 feet until under a conspicuous, right-facing dihedral that shoots straight up about 100 feet. Work up to a huge roof and move 8 feet left and up and arrive at a belay stance with a bolt. The remainder goes up the obvious dihedral.

Practice Climb Number 101. 5.12? First ascent in 1966 by Larry and Roger Dalke. Free ascent of the 1st pitch in 1976 by David Breashears, Steve Wunsch, and Jim Erickson. Free lead of 2nd pitch in 1981 by John Allen. Find the start of Side Wall. Immediately left (north) is a steep, narrow face (buttress). Free-climb to an inside-corner and work 60(?) feet up to a ledge belay. The 2nd pitch is much harder and ascends the overhang above (on the left), then works to a ledge belay.

John Allen suggested the "free" name for this route: "Practice For What?"

Pony Express (with direct start). 5.11a? First ascent in 1966 by Larry and Roger Dalke. Free ascent in 1974 by Duncan Ferguson, Steve Wunsch, and John Bragg. The original 1st lead of this was done via the first part of Mesca-Line and then up a shallow, left-facing dihedral. Subsequent parties found a more direct start that is recommended and here included. The first large buttress north of the Long John Wall (and still part of the West Ridge) is the Mail Ridge. About 60 or more feet left (north) of the Mail Ridge Route is a smooth wall with a tree on a ledge about 75 feet up. The tree is at the base of a prominent, right-facing dihedral. This prominent dihedral is the route. Climb straight up a steep wall (5.9) just right of a crack, to the tree. The crux 2nd pitch ascends the classic dihedral (moving partly left of the dihedral, or staying directly in the dihedral which is more difficult).

Iron Horse. 5.11c (serious). First ascent in 1984 by Dan Michael, Jim Michael, and Dan Hare. The 1st pitch parallels the 1st pitch of Pony Express via thin cracks just to the right. The next pitch does the crux of Pony Express, then climbs the arete left of the corner past a bolt. Mostly climb left of the arete.

Kashmir. 5.11b or c. First ascent in 1979 by Charlie Fowler. This is simply another example of the excellent short climbs found in abundance on the West Ridge. Walk far up along the West Ridge until just below (south) of where the ridge is broken by a large talus gully. Look for a thin, finger-tip crack in an almost vertical wall, just right of an easy hand-jam crack. The finger-tip crack leads to a tree on a ledge.

The Rincon Wall.

This is the large cliff on the southwest side of Shirt Tail Peak. It is actually the upper extension of the West Ridge, although separated from the West Ridge by a large scree gully. Rincon is the largest, southwest-facing wall high on the mountain to the north -- as seen from where the road crosses the river near Supremacy Slab. Approach by starting up the Walker Ranch trail, then cut northeast.

Rincon. 5.10d or 5.11a. First ascent in 1962 by Layton Kor and Jack Turner. Free ascent in 1969 by Jim Erickson and Dave Meyers.

Named after a surfing area in California. Near the center of the Rincon Wall is a fantastic, 300-foot, right-facing dihedral that slants upward and slightly right. Start at the lowest point along the base of the wall. The 1st lead is one of the most beautiful in the area and ascends a perfect hand/finger-crack (5.10a) in a smooth, near-vertical slab. Belay atop the crack, on a stance at the start of the actual dihedral. Move up and slightly right, traverse left to the top of a huge flake in the dihedral, and continue up the dihedral (5.8) to a belay stance. The final pitch starts with a band of red, broken rock. Then surmount the crux bulge in the dihedral. The protection and climbing are difficult. Arrive at a huge ledge which can be followed up and west, around a corner, and downward west to the scree.

Center Route. 5.11a. First ascent in 1964 by Larry and Roger Dalke. Free ascent in 1976 by Chris Reveley, Scott Woodruff, and Dan Hare. This ascends the first very steep crack left of Rincon, the first and best pitch starting with a short overhang, moving up a face just east of a right-facing dihedral, surmounting a short roof to the left, and ascending a crux finger-tip crack up a steep wall.

Wendego. 5.12. First ascent in 1964 by Pat Ament and Larry Dalke. Free ascent of 1st lead in 1980 by Jeff Achey, Kevin Bein, and Barbara Devine. Complete free ascent in 1981 by Jeff Achey and Leonard Coyne. The route ascends the bulging wall left (west) of Center Route, starting up a prominent, right-leaning (overhanging) dihedral. The dihedral is the crux, with the hardest single move found very near the bottom. Where the rock becomes vertical, at the top of the dihedral, continue up to a virtually hanging belay. From here, traverse right (around a corner) to the next crack and follow it. The remainder of the route will be found.

Aerial Book. 5.11b. First ascent in 1965 by Pat Ament and Fred Pfahler. Free ascent in 1975 by Wendell Nuss and Mike Gilbert. A short distance uphill west from the right-leaning dihedral of Wendego, find a classic dihedral (originally used to teach a friend direct-aid). Climb this obvious dihedral about 45 feet (stemming, with handholds hard to find). The 2nd pitch, easier to protect but more difficult, traverses right, to a tree and ascends a strenuous finger-crack.

Over The Hill. 5.10a or b. First ascent in 1972 by Pat Ament, Jim Erickson, and Bill Putnam. Just left (west) of Aerial Book is a 150-foot, classic dihedral similar to Aerial Book but not as deep. Start up the dihedral and reach the top of a large block. Now the dihedral becomes smoother and steeper. Continue up this section and onward to a belay ledge with a small tree. The 2nd pitch ascends the next short dihedral on small holds. Exit the dihedral up and left to a big, rocky ledge. The final pitch was done in the rain on the first ascent. Start with the obvious dihedral above the ledge, via a thin crack, and soon move right, onto the smooth, "diamond" face, and up its sleek, obvious finger-crack system.

Cadillac Crag.

This is a series of south-facing buttresses or aretes (cadillac fins) located in the forest about 150 yards west and slightly uphill from the Rincon Wall. Many good routes exist.

Highway Of Diamonds. 5.9+. First ascent in 1973 by Steve Wunsch, Bob Hritz, and Jim Logan. This route ascends the fin or arete that is the second from the right (if you are facing north). Climb easily up 25-30 feet, hand-traverse left along a wide crack. Angle up left across a 5.8 face. Go up a thin-ish crack into a small, left-facing corner. Then move out and left to a belay on the edge. Work upward to a roof and around it on the right (the crux). Continue up the edge.

Supremacy Rock.

This quartzite formation, diamond-shaped into a couple of excellent small summits, is located above the river, on the south side of the road, just before the bridge (about a mile up the road from the ranger's toll booth).

Supremacy Slab. 5.9+. No one knows who made the first ascent or the first leading ascent, although Royal Robbins certainly led it in 1964 without bolts and perhaps only one piton. On an earlier attempt, Jim McCarthy took a leader fall and was stopped by the rope. He pulled out a bolt, turned head first, and broke his thumb on the ground. The route goes more or less up the middle of the shiny, larger quartzite slab that faces north. Start by angling a few feet up and right, then up and left. Follow a clear, delicate crack up and right about 35 or 40 feet, with a scarcity of handholds, to where it is easy to move up and left.

Supremacy Crack. 5.11b. First ascent (top-rope) in 1965 by Pat Ament. Led in 1966 by Pat Ament. This was the first of its kind in the area, an overhanging hand-crack of 5.11 difficulty. The route is located on the overhanging (south) side of Supremacy.

Pat Ament on Supremacy Crack, 1975 -- photo by Tom Frost

The Web. 5.13. First ascent in 1986 by Chris Hill and Christian Griffith. Protected by a line of rappel-placed bolts, this strenuous sport-climb goes up the overhanging, golden wall left (west) of Supremacy Crack.

Milton Boulder.

This rock is on the north side of the road, about halfway between the Bastille and Supremacy Slab. The name "Milton" was painted on the south wall at the time the well-known Milton Boulder route was done, in 1968, by Pat Ament up the steep, south wall, passing a small, white crystal (used by the right hand) and attaining a sloping ledge at the top.

Nothing's Impossible. B2. First ascent in 1985, by a run and jump to the top by six-foot-siven Jimmy Ratzlaff. Climbed free in 1986, in conventional style, by Steve Mammen. This is an astonishing problem up the vertical, slightly concave, right portion of the south wall.

Peanuts Wall.

Many routes, and several good routes, exist on this gray and yellow, north-facing, triangular-shaped wall high on the south side of Eldorado Canyon between the Bastille and Supremacy Slab. The best approach is by starting at a parking spot just east of Supremacy and walking east along the old Bastille road (now a trail). Break off the path and up the talus in a southeasterly, diagonal fashion.

Star Wars. 5.8+. First ascent in 1977 by Kevin Donald and students, a route pioneered by one of the founders of Eldorado's Alpine School (the school is no longer based in Eldorado). This is one of the nicer lines on the Peanuts Wall. Up along the right side of the wall (the lower Peanuts Wall), it is possible to spot the obvious, northwest-facing hand-crack that forms the main challenge. One approach to the crack is to wander up broken rock below it. Another climbs a short headwall off the ground. The best perhaps is to scramble from the west, onto a ledge, and then east along a big ledge to the start. The route is two pitches, one (5.6) up a type of dihedral-crack that rises above the big ledge. The 2nd pitch (the crux) goes straight up a difficult, slightly off-size hand-jam. The crack makes a short, tricky turn to right after which is found a deep dihedral/crack (moderate). Descend by first scrambling up the summit ridge to the southwest. Find a gully with trees leading down west.

The Empire Strikes Back. 5.10+. First ascent of 1st pitch in 1980 by Mike Brooks and Chip Ruckgaber. Free ascent of the 2nd pitch led by Dan Michael. This route parallels Star Wars to the right. Begin at a left-facing dihedral. Climb the dihedral (5.9). Go up the dihedral above before moving left and through a notch (5.10+).

The Sacred And The Profane. 5.12d or 5.13a? First ascent in 1986 led by Dale Goddard. This is a sport-climb (with three bolts) usually top-roped but led by Goddard. The route goes up the blunt arete near the center of the lower part of the Peanuts Wall. Move over a roof with a bolt. Generally follow the right side of the arete.

Just Another Girl's Climb. 5.12a or b. First ascent in 1987 by Andrea Azoff and Charlie Fowler. About 100 feet or more up on the right side from the lowest part of the Peanuts Wall, find this lovely, difficult wall. Climb to a roof that is strenuous (protected by a bolt). The face above is followed, with bolts for protection (widely spaced), until a steep traverse left is made.

The Mickey Mouse (called also Red Dihedral Wall).

This wall faces southwest, high above Eldorado to the south, on a formation whose summit has two "ears." One approach to the rock is by driving to Coal Creek Canyon (south of Eldorado) and following a dirt road north until the railroad tracks are met, at which point it is possible to walk north along the tracks (through four exhilarating tunnels). Another approach is to hike directly up the mountainside, starting near the old entrance to Eldorado (in the vicinity of the Post Office).

Tunnel Vision. 5.13a. First ascent led in 1991 by Colin Lantz. This is the very close to the tunnel (just west and above the track). Look for a bolted, south-facing wall near a tree.
TGV. 5.13c. First led in 1992 by George Squibb. Bolts were placed by other parties, and many tried this classically overhanging sport-route prior to Squibb's ascent. The route ascends the right side of a huge, south-facing roof, not far up (west) above the railroad tunnel at the bottom of the wall.
The Red Dihedral. 5.12+? First ascent in 1964 by Layton Kor, Paul Mayrose, and Larry Dalke. Free ascent in 1985 by Christian Griffith and Eric Doub. This dihedral is the most obvious, striking feature of the entire Mickey Mouse. The 1st pitch works up a steep, 80-foot lieback jam-crack to a large shelf. The 2nd lead goes straight up the obvious rock to a ledge below the fantastic, overhanging, red dihedral. The 3rd lead (first 15 foot section) is the most difficult and climbs the dihedral. The 4th pitch finishes the dihedral and traverses left, under an obvious roof. For those that think sport-climbing is always safe, Christian Griffith recalls, "Rushing in the late day to make a clip, I took a 40-foot fall and pulled one of Kor's bolts. I have the bolt hanging on my wall." There are now a number of bolts on the route that were not placed by the first ascent party.

Layton Kor at the top of the Red Dihedral, 1964 -- photo by Paul Mayrose

Perilous Journey. 5.11a or b? (protection imaginary). First ascent in 1975 by David Breashears and Steve Mammen. A short walk up along the Mickey Mouse, and a short distance right (east) of an obvious left-facing dihedral, find the impressive, steep wall (slab) that is done in a single, unprotected pitch. The crux is found about 35-40 feet above the ground.

David Breashears finishes Perilous Journey / photo by Pat Ament

Krystal Klyr. 5.11a or b? (no protection, but for one dubious point half way up). First ascent in 1975 by David Breashears, Steve Mammen, and Jim Collins. Not far left of Perilous Journey and just right (east) of a kind of arete is this impressive route. Up on the wall a short distance is a white crystal that is a crucial hold. The route climbs over a small roof to a flake, where perhaps some type of protection can be set, then ascends a vertical headwall. There are two crux sections, both delicate, strenuous face-climbing.

Perversion. 5.9 or 5.10. First ascent in 1963 by Layton Kor, Paul Mayrose, Charles Kemp, and Bob Bradley. Free ascent in 1974 by Roger Briggs and Larry Hamilton. This was done by two parties of two. The two ropes started separately but became one party about halfway up the wall. As a result, there are two variations to start:

Variation 1. Amusement. 5.8. (Mayrose, Bradley). Start about 150 feet left and uphill from the start of the Red Dihedral. Follow a small, left-facing inside-corner.

Variation 2. Abusement. 5.10. (Kor, Kemp, free by Briggs, Hamilton). About 40 feet left of Amusement, climb beautiful finger-cracks for two pitches. From the ledge where the two variations join, scramble up and climb inside-corners and cracks (5.7) to the base of a large, inside-corner. After an 80-foot lieback up this inside-corner, traverse right, around a prominent roof, and reach the top. The upper portion of this route ascends to the left of a large slab that is easily seen from the ground.

Captain Beyond. 5.10. First ascent in 1974 by Roger and Bill Briggs. Combined with Abusement, this is a long, classic route. From the top of Abusement, go up and then angle left into a difficult chimney and off-width crack.

Beginner's Mind. 5.11+. First ascent in 1981 by Jeff Achey and Mark Sonnenfeld. This is an obvious crack (thin) that is a direct start to Captain Beyond. Begin a short distance (a few feet) left of that route. Jeff Achey suggests, "Bring a number 4 crack 'n up and be prepared to fall on it!"

Better Red Than Dead. 5.12b. First ascent in 1985 by Dan Michael and Mark Sonnenfeld. An example of the many sport-climbs now present on the Mickey Mouse (Red Dihedral Wall). This starts roughly 15 feet left of Beginner's Mind, about 30 feet right of Scorpius, and is a sport-climb with questionable "red" bolts. From a roof, move left to Scorpius and find a dihedral.

Scorpius. 5.11?. First ascent in 1981 by Jeff Achey and Robert Palais. This route has a unique history. Achey recalls, "Thin pitons were hand-placed for protection!" The route climbs the bulging wall left of Beginner's Mind. Start left of that route and right of the easy start to Perversion, on a flake-ledge. Climb a shallow groove, then go up and right (under a small roof). Work generally up and right, then left to a prominent crack with a bush. Reach a large ledge.

THE AUTHORS

Cleve McCarty is a Boulder dentist and Denver son. He and his wife Jackie have raised six children. Cleve's photography is now being shown in Denver, Milwaukee, and Houston. His favorite family excursion was the single day, 1977 bicycle trip from Boulder to the Longs Peak ranger station and then an ascent of Kiener's up the east face of Longs with his then 12-year-old son Eric, and back on bike to Boulder in the evening. One memorable ascent was the intricate spiral route of the Guglia di Brenta in the Italian Dolomites with his son Eric in 1988. His glaciated peak excursions include Waddington, Robson, Assininboine, and the second American team ascent of the Cassin Ridge of Mt. McKinley.

Tom Frost writes, "Pat Ament is the premier author of the American climbing scene by virtue of the number of books and essays and the quality of writing. He has written the biographies of no less measure of men than John Gill and Royal Robbins." Six of Pat's articles have been selected for international anthologies of best climbing writings. Author of twenty books, he has had approximately one hundred articles published in various mountaineering journals. As a writer, his most serious study is poetry. Poems of his have been published in literary journals. He did the first climbs of a 5.11 grade in Colorado, the first 5.11 in Yosemite, was a pioneer of difficult bouldering, and has been a prolific mentor. Described as "an eclectic man," in Climbing Magazine, he is a member of the black belt council of Shotokan Karate of America, a chess expert, an artist, photographer, and pianist, now also a husband and father.

INDEX OF CIIMBS AND CLIMBER NAMES

A FEW SUGGESTIONS FOR SAFETY

1. Don't climb below other parties. People drop equipment and knock rocks off. A climb will always wait for another day.

2. Do not trust sling webbing or other sling cord found in place. Webbing (and rope) is affected by the sun. It weathers and weakens.

3. Always use at least two anchors to rappel, unless the anchor is a large, solid, well-rooted tree or a huge, steel eyebolt.

4. Do not assume that climbs of a 5.5 to 5.8 grade are appropriate for beginners. Even with the high standard of today's climbers, beginners are vulnerable and have a lot to learn. A climb such as the Bulge, for example, is 5.8 but has the potential for a long, dangerous swing on the rope should the second climber fall.

5. A leader should place protection for the second climber on traverses, even if the leader does not feel the need for protection.

6. Do not trust your whole life to one of the single old bolts that are often encountered in the area. Some of the original bolts were placed as marginal protection or for supporting no more than body weight. Back up such bolts with added protection. The same is true for fixed pitons. Unless you have a hammer and can test a piton found already in place, it should be suspect. Pitons often weaken and loosen in cracks over the years.

7. Be alert for signs of bad weather. Develop a keen sense for retreating before storms build up or avoiding places exposed to lightning.

8. Beware of guidebook errors. Every guide is likely to have at least a few.

9. If starting late, bring a pocket flashlight for anchoring in the dark.